UNCOMMON FATHERS

Reflections on Raising a Child with a Disability

Edited by Donald J. Meyer

WOODBINE HOUSE 1995

All rights reserved under International and Pan-American copyright conventions. Published in the United States of America by Woodbine House, Inc., 6510 Bells Mill Rd., Bethesda, MD 20817. 800–843–7323.

Cover illustration: Phil Hocking

Library of Congress Cataloging-in-Publication Data

Uncommon fathers : reflections on raising a child with a disability / edited by Donald J. Meyer.

   p.   cm.

  ISBN 0–933149–68–9

  1. Parents of handicapped children—United States—Case studies. 2. Fathers—United States—Case studies. 3. Fathers—United States—Psychology. 4. Father and child—United States—Case studies. I. Meyer, Donald J. (Donald Joseph), 1951–

HQ759.913.U53 1995   95–8651

649'.152—dc20   CIP

Manufactured in the United States of America

10 9 8 7 6 5 4 3

To my parents,
the Rev. Mr. Ferd C. and Adele P. Meyer

Table of Contents

Preface

my father moved through dooms of love
through sames of am through haves of give
singing each morning out of each night
my father moved through depths of height
　　　　　　　　　　—E.E. Cummings

My son, Jay is 16 and moderately retarded. I think
the most important question is not "What is
mental retardation?" It is "What does mental
retardation mean? What does it do to us?"
　　　　　　　　　　—Rud Turnbull

It was a lonely epiphany.
　　　　　　　　　—Al Gore, describing the
　　　　　　　　　time following his son's
　　　　　　　　　accident

I sat in my advisor's office, new to the Northwest,
new to graduate school, awed and intimidated by the institution and my advisor. Dr. Hayden (few dared to call
her Alice) was a pioneer in early intervention, and was
somewhat of a legend. When I met her in 1978, she was
well past the University's official retirement age, but she
still advised students—if what she gave could be called
advice.

I had always thought of advice as counsel for a person to take or leave. Not so with Dr. Hayden. She wanted the University of Washington's Experimental Education Unit to have a program for fathers of infants with disabilities. And, because I was the only early childhood special education graduate student who happened to be male, Dr. Hayden "advised" me to be part of it. "We need to do something about these fathers!" she announced. (Like so many other efforts to reach out to parents, the University's earlier attempts to create a program for parents had resulted in a program for mothers.)

I was delighted with my assignment. As a teacher, I had enjoyed the company of parents and "doing something about these fathers" sounded both novel and needed. Largely making it up as we went along, Greg Schell—a father of a child with Down syndrome—and I began planning the first meetings of our Fathers Program.

"Fathers?!" we were warned by our classmates and colleagues, "They never show up. When they do, they don't say anything!" To recruit men for the Fathers Program, Greg and I decided to try a Fathers Only Workshop at a nearby early intervention center. It did not begin auspiciously. Only three fathers showed up. With hands in their pockets, they looked at the walls with an expression that seemed to say "Why the hell did I let my wife talk me into coming to this?" We looked at the clock: 7 p.m. The workshop was supposed to go until 9:30. What on earth could the five of us possibly talk about for two and one-half hours?

Our concerns, of course, were without merit. The conversation started slowly with one brave father describing his family's experiences, his views on life with a child who has a disability. As he spoke, the other fathers had what we would later call "aha!" experiences: "I can't believe that happened to you too!" they said, "Let me tell you what happened to us." As they discussed their children, their wives, and their families, they quickly learned that they were not alone with their joys and concerns. Finding much common ground, the conversation snowballed. We ended the workshop at 10:30 and could have gone on longer.

This was not an isolated experience. During the eight years that we ran the Fathers Program, participants met twice a month to share frustration, information, and knowing laughs. Although their only common denominator was that they had children with disabilities, the men understood one another in a way that a coworker, best friend, or brother could not.

On occasion, we would run Fathers Only Workshops at national conferences. Participants—sometimes as many as 100–would exchange insights and war stories and validate each other's experiences. Often, the din of the conversation was such that we were asked "to keep it down" by presenters in neighboring rooms. Fathers became so involved in talking to their peers that we sometimes needed to shoo them out of the room at the end of the meetings and encourage them to continue their conversations in the lobby or at a nearby bar. All this from fathers who "don't say anything." Clearly these men have much to say, and much to offer one another.

In *Uncommon Fathers,* readers who are fathers will meet peers. They will develop a broader understanding of their own situation as authors share their views, concerns, and hard-earned joys. Fathers will find others who, like Rud Turnbull, search for the meaning in disability. Unlike Al Gore's, their epiphanies will not be revelations made in isolation.

Although the primary audience for *Uncommon Fathers* is other fathers of children with special needs, it would be regrettable if the readership ended there. Mothers who would like insight into what keeps their husbands up at night will benefit from the often achingly candid testimony of these men. Social workers, special educators, family counselors, therapists, academicians, researchers, and policy makers who wish to reform systems that treat fathers as "the other parent"—an afterthought—will do well to learn how these men strive to be vital participants in their children's lives and education.

The uncommon fathers represented in this book are a diverse group: Included are students, artists, teachers, a Christian missionary, a retired police officer, businessmen, attorneys, government workers, a rabbi, writers, a parole officer, and full-time activists, writing from locales ranging from upstate New York to Tokyo. Their children—ages 4 to 28 years—have autism, Down syndrome, cerebral palsy, hydrocephalus, hearing impairments, as well as undiagnosed disabilities that range from mild to severe.

The essays in *Uncommon Fathers* are arranged according to the age of the authors' children to give readers a perspective of how fathers' issues can change over time. These men were asked to comment on the time of diagnosis if they wished, but to focus primarily on here-and-now: *What do you find yourself thinking about as you drive to work, take a shower, or mow the lawn?*

In the end, the request to contribute to this book was patently unfair. In the space of approximately ten or so typewritten pages, contributors were asked to reflect upon topics that are among the most subjective, personal, and elusive imaginable: *How did you learn of your child's diagnosis? What was your reaction? Was this different from the child's mother's reaction? How did other family members react? How has your perception of disabilities changed over time? Do you have concerns about your typically developing children? How has being the father of a child with special needs changed your life? How has it changed your view of your work? Has it changed your philosophy of life? Has it changed how you relate to your family? When you think about your child's future, what do you see? Along the way, what has helped? What didn't help? What advice would you have for schools and other agencies to assure that fathers are "brought into the loop"? What advice would you have for a father who just learned that his child has a disability?* Despite this most difficult request, these men opened their hearts, minds, and souls to offer insights into a family member rarely described in any form of literature—popular, clinical, or research.

Readers will find that the opinions and experiences of fathers of children with special needs are anything but monolithic. As might be expected from such a diverse group of men, the authors hold differing religious and philosophical interpretations of their children's disabilities. They possess a wide range of coping strategies. Some are upbeat and optimistic; others are still struggling; most are somewhere in-between. Despite their differences, recurring themes and common threads emerge from the essays of these uncommon men. Like E. E.

Cummings's father, their passion, love, and commitment to their children and families move them through profound *depths of height, sames of am,* and *haves of give.* Each, in his own way, is determined to *sing each morning out of each night.* Their families are lucky to have these men in their lives; we are lucky to have their thoughts.

Acknowledgments

It is a pleasure to have a chance to thank those who have helped me transform *Uncommon Fathers* from an idea into a reality. I am indebted to:

Martha Blue-Banning, Betsy Santelli, Patricia Oelwein, Margaret Lewis, and Jenny Waldon-Weaver for introducing me to some of the fathers whom readers will meet in this book;

Tizzy Bennett and Susan Macek of Seattle's Children's Hospital and Medical Center for their unfailing support of my work;

Greg Schell and the other members of the Fathers Program for teaching me about the fathers' unique joys and concerns and, in the process, influencing my career in significant and satisfying ways;

The staff at Woodbine House for their enthusiasm—from the very start—for this project;

Patricia Vadasy, valued friend and co-author, for being a superb sounding board;

Patricia Lott and Erica Erickson of the Sibling Support Project for their keen insight and assistance during the preparation of this manuscript; and

Terese Marie De Leonardis, my wife, and Gina, Angela, Tony, and Rosie, our children, for cheerfully tolerating my unconventional—but always rewarding—career.

Of course, this book would not exist without the men who generously agreed to share their lives with us in these pages. I am especially grateful for their contributions.

Creating Answers

Bob Dale

In February of 1990 my daughter, Jessica, was a happy, healthy seven-month-old, pulling up and walking along the edge of the sofa, smiling a smile so bright and beautiful that angels were envious; she stole every heart she touched. Today Jessica lies virtually motionless on her back—deaf, blind, and paralyzed, but still smiling that angelic smile and displaying the nature of the unimpaired beauty that was born to us.

Jessica had spinal meningitis. We live in a small, rural Missouri farming community, and our health care system isn't the best in the world. What could have been cured with a round of antibiotics went undetected, and, as a consequence, many lives were changed.

After four years, the questions "why my baby?" "why me?" and "why aren't You answering my prayers?" have become commonplace and even a little boring. But I still find myself asking them. Slowly, I am creating answers. My answers are not divine in nature, or inspired in content. They are comprised of meanings that I have picked; they are purely subjective, unsubstantiated by data, but they are mine and they work.

It is devastating to be told that your daughter will be as affected as this. It is even tougher when that incessant historical record in your head keeps reminding you that it could have been avoided *if only.* . . . It is tough.

When I hold Jessica, I look into her eyes wanting to see that same sweet, smiling baby that used to crawl to me. The truth is that baby is gone. I now have another baby, one who will be my baby for the rest of her life. Jessica depends on us for everything: food, water, medicines, clean clothes, recreation. She even needs us to turn her over in bed during the night. The amazing thing is this: I need her more than she needs me.

Jessica has taught me what true love is. Poets and preachers, young lovers, and idealists have professed a knowledge of this elusive concept for years. But, in Jessica's silence, I have learned the real essence of love: you give everything and expect nothing in return.

Even husbands and wives give kisses expecting kisses in return. Not so with Jesse. You give for the pure love of it, knowing that she is unable to reciprocate. You watch her face as you tend to her, looking for any sign of pleasure or happiness, and when you catch a glimpse, real or imagined, you repeat what you were doing, because you found something that makes her happy. The joy of loving her is its own reward. This could quite possibly be the purest love I've ever felt, untainted by worldly expectations, unaffected by demands, cause or effect. It simply surrounds you.

Jessica has taught me a Positive Human Inventory system, wherein one first takes stock of all a person is and can do, and deficits are relegated to the rear for secondary consideration and later remediation. In the Positive Human Inventory, the first thing you note when you encounter a human is that they have life. Life is a precious gift to be cherished and nurtured the best way you know how. It is not some elusive dream, nor is it to be taken for granted and wasted. Life is not some fragile vase to be perched on a pedestal to exist in a vacuum of artifacts. Life is to be lived—risks and all.

When people ask, "Why spend all that money, time, and effort to keep her alive . . . what 'quality' can her life have, anyway?", I have to shake my head and pity their ignorance. Jessica has taught me that life doesn't *have* quality, life *is* quality.

Life's quality is contagious. Where it seems that some people enjoy a "better" quality of life, in truth they may simply be better than others at appreciating their own intrinsic value. (If you observe you will notice that these people tend to surround themselves with others who possess these same attributes.)

Jessica has taught me to open my eyes to the world, to see its many faces. We have people on this planet who do not seem to realize that people like Jessica are humans, who have rights, families, and feelings. Unfortunately, many of these people are employed by the very organizations mandated to fulfill the needs of people in Jessica's condition. At first, I thought their mandate was to drive me crazy, until I realized that my mandate was to learn to understand *them*, and help them learn what I have learned from Jessica. Once I learned to look at service providers this way, I began to realize that most providers can be wonderful to work with—despite the fact that I'm just a father.

Being a father usually assigns one to a second-class status in the family. Mothers are thought of as the norm when it comes to dealing with kids with special needs. Early on, I found out that my presence wasn't needed or even wanted at many of the meetings and staffings regarding Jessica. Once, after answering a social worker's questions, I was thanked for my cooperation and informed that the worker would check my answers with my wife for accuracy. I found this very curious, especially since the questions dealt with my work record and employment history.

It would be easy to step aside and let my wife take charge of these activities. After all, stepping aside was the message sent loudly and clearly to me from many places. But my wife couldn't deal with this trauma alone. It took two of us to handle all that was happening; service providers would just have to get to know me and learn to accept, if not like, the fact that I was involved with my daughter's life. I learned their rules and studied the laws governing the various agencies and departments and set out to get all the help Jessica needed to optimize her life.

Four years later, battle-scarred, war-toughened and wiser for the experiences, I still find immeasurable joy in holding my angelic child and coaxing her into a grin. And when the rough spots hit—and they hit relentlessly—I simply take a deep breath, ask myself who is really suffering, and then do what has to be done.

Becoming actively involved with my daughter's rehabilitation has been my main coping mechanism. When Jessica was lying comatose in the hospital I was overwhelmed by a sickening sense of helplessness. There were nurses, doctors, specialists from disciplines that I did not know even existed, technicians, and others, diligently attending to her, and all I could do was sit back and watch. I could stay awake and touch her hand, and be with her while she faced death, but I could not *do* anything! I had to realize that while I may be a good father, I am not a super power.

I cannot know everything there is to know about Jessica's neurological impairments. Neither can the doctors. That's why we have so many specialists. But, what I *can* do is participate in her life. I can attend the meetings and the conferences to make sure that her needs are being met. I can educate myself enough to understand the jargon, and to know what options exist for her.

And by doing so I have learned to appreciate things that heretofore have escaped my notice. When I see a child in a wheelchair, I see a kid who is probably as fascinated by cartoons as my nine-year-old. I no longer hear the distorted speech of a person with cerebral palsy; I recognize the effort and courage it took for that person to learn to speak so well. I see a man playing with his little boy who is hearing impaired. Watching as they sign to one another, I realize that they simply crossed the bridge to another form of communication. The boy is whole, perfect, and loved. So what if he can't hear! Jessica is a part of this world and a large part of my life, and she is whole and perfect and loved.

It seems a contradiction to refer to a person who is deaf, blind, and quadriplegic as perfect, but one has to assume that if the universe is indeed unfolding as it should, then being deaf, blind, and quadriplegic is to be part of it. It is, therefore, as it should be. After all, where is it written that in order to be a viable member of the human race you must have the following list of standard equipment: hands-2, legs-2 (working), eyes-2 (sighted), IQ-70 (minimum) and so on?

Don't get me wrong—if miracles could happen, and if one of them was tossed Jessica's way, I would be ecstatic. I'm not happy that my daughter has lost her healthy life, her ability to grow and develop typically. Every time I see a little four-year-old, blond-haired girl playing, walking with her daddy, pleading with him to buy her an ice cream, I realize a deep and painful sense of loss. I feel cheated and misused.

But as quickly as these feelings come, they are replaced by a sense of wonder at the beauty of this work of art, this healthy child. I smile and say a silent prayer asking God to follow that child closely and to protect her. My child is waiting for me at home, and she likes ice cream, too.

When we left the hospital four years ago, Jessica's resident told us that we would probably wake up one morning to find that Jesse had choked on her own saliva in the middle of the night and had died. Consequently, if she merely sighed heavily I sat straight up in bed and kept vigil until dawn.

I wish I could say that I have learned to sleep better over the years. The resident's well-meaning, but ill-advised prediction no longer keeps me awake, but the amount of homework I have to do takes a lot more time than I bargained for.

You see, while we were new to all this, we looked for psychological support, a counselor, a parent support group, or something to help us during these tough times. We found nothing. This prompted me to go back to college to work on an advanced degree in psychological counseling. Along the way, I have helped start three parent support groups. These activities are themselves coping strategies.

Am I in denial and using these other activities to hide from the reality of Jessica's condition? At first, most assuredly so. But, as time passed, I went about the business of helping Jesse and other children with disabilities. Learning and growing myself, I learned to see positive aspects in each situation. I learned to take the bad in stride, and not to blame the world for my misfortune. I managed to take a monumental amount of psychological insults and harsh realities and—one by one—incorporate them into my way of life. If I had attempted to acclimate myself to all these things at once, I would have surely gone mad.

None of us are powerless. All of us have assets upon which to draw that can enhance our children's lives and our own with them. Your strengths may differ from mine, but rest assured, they are there. You can make your child's life better, regardless of his or her level of involvement.

Most fathers are told to do the same thing I was: be strong for your family. Sometimes I don't feel very strong. Sometimes I'm tired and want all of it to go away. Sometimes I cry. I let my two boys know they can cry, too. Sometimes we cry together.

I encourage my sons, ages six and nine, to ask questions about Jessica, and to express their feelings about her. About a year ago, I was surprised to discover that Devon, then five years old, didn't realize that she had any problems. She was lying on her mat in the den, and Devon was crawling around her on the floor. I asked him what he was doing. He replied that he was teaching Jessica to crawl. His teacher said that you have to crawl before you can walk. I asked him if he knew why Jessica couldn't walk, and he said that it was because she was still a baby. To Devon, who wasn't quite three years old when Jesse was put in the hospital, she was still as she was three years earlier: a baby.

Devon didn't comprehend the severity of Jessica's illness. He didn't understand how close to death she had come. All he knew was that Jessica and his parents left for a couple of months, and that he and Zachary had to live with Grandma and Grandpa while we were gone.

Devon and I sat together while I explained the grim realities of Jessica's illness to him. He asked questions, mostly about how to play with her. Then he curled up on the mat next to her, put his arm around her, stuck his thumb in his mouth and fell asleep. He knew the truth now, but it didn't matter.

Zachary was just turning five when all this happened. He was young enough to not fully comprehend, but old enough to experience a sense of loss and separation. Over the years he has asked many questions about her life, limitations, and perceptions. I'm always careful to take time to discuss these matters at whatever length he determines to be appropriate. Sometimes he wants a quick answer; other times he wants to sit and fully discuss things.

It is important for Zachary to explore these issues, because next to Jesse, it is Zachary who has suffered the most. I feel fortunate that Zachary and I have a strong relationship. He knows that my love for him is boundless. Without knowing what was happening to him, he was taken from his home to his grandparents', and put in a day care facility full of kids he had never seen before. Grandma and Grandpa tried to explain what was happening and why his mother and I had to be away. He accepted it, but he didn't like it. And, though he knew he was loved, he became terribly confused.

After we finally returned home, the many other changes exacerbated his confusion. Why were we so tired all the time? Why can't we go out for dinner? Why can't I have that new toy? Why are you spending so much time with Jessica? The questions were valid and numerous.

This posed another challenge: How do you explain to a five-year-old that he has to put his needs on hold, because his sister's are more pressing? Or, in the alternative, how do you take care of Jessica, and Zachary, and Devon and Robbie and yourself without blowing a gasket?

Over the years we have devised an answer: we escape! I arrange for help with Jessica from whatever resources are available and plan a time to do something with the rest of the family. I think the operative word here is *plan*.

Since having a child with many health care needs effectively eliminates spontaneity, these events have to be planned several weeks in advance. However, planning the activity seems to give the boys something to look forward to, while reinforcing in their minds that they are as important as Jessica. After we figure out what we want to do, I go to work to assure that Jesse's needs are all covered. Then we spend the next week or so talking to the boys about what we are going to do, and how we are going to do it.

I've been planning these "escape" trips with the boys for about a year now, and I have noticed tremendous changes in their attitudes. They need a time when *their* special needs can be met. Sometimes we go to the zoo, and sometimes we check into a motel to utilize an indoor pool. We may take in a movie, or spend the afternoon at Chuckee Cheez's. But whatever we do, it is the boys who come first with no sister to steal the limelight. I think this strategy has helped our sons become more tolerant of the time their mother and I spend with Jessica.

Jessica is a positive influence on her brothers as well. One day a little girl from the special education classroom became lost and a little disoriented on the playground. She couldn't find her way and was frightened. Several of the little boys in Zach's class gathered around her and started taunting her, saying "Oooh, retard! Don't touch her or you'll get retard germs," etc. When Zachary saw what was happening, he walked up and gently took the little girl by the arm, looked at his classmates and said, "I don't know why you're treating her like this. She's just like us, but she has special needs. She has feelings, though." And with that, he led her to her appointed place and went back to his playing.

The teachers who reported this incident to me were amazed at his sensitivity, sincerity, and sheer guts. The next day he was presented with a certificate from the STAR club saying, "Zachary Dale Gives Good Advice." He didn't know what it was for. After all, he was only doing what he thought was right. Am I proud? Pardon me, while I sew the buttons back on my shirt.

How do I characterize my relationship with Jessica? I don't know. You need to realize that Jesse is not expected to live much past the age of twelve or thirteen, so every moment with her is a precious gift; a golden point in time to be savored. Every smile is a prayer answered.

Every time I stroke her cheek I feel a sense of wonder and appreciation that she is here, with me now.

Because of Jessica, I have increased my awareness of people with disabilities. I have become educated in many areas of policy and law, and I have attended over fifty I.E.P. meetings, other than hers, to help other kids get the most out of their education. Because of her I have met hundreds of parents, and talked at length with them about the challenges they face raising their child with special needs. I have lobbied our state legislature for Jessica, and, together with hundreds of other parents, helped to effect positive change in the state of Missouri. Because of Jessica I have helped to raise the level of awareness on the part of state officials and educators. All because of a little four-year-old girl.

She has literally shaken the world. Who among us can say the same thing?

Bob Dale is the father of three children, Zachary, age 9, Devon, age 6, and Jessica, age 4, all residing in Portageville, Missouri. Bob has become a well-known advocate for children with disabilities in Missouri. He has been active with Southeast Missouri Deaf Services, Missouri Parents Act (MPACT), The Parent Action Coalition, and others. He has been honored as Region Nine Council on Developmental Disabilities' Volunteer of the Year, Beta Sigma Phi's Man of the Year, and has been named an Outstanding Young Man in America. Bob has presented at state, national, and international conferences. Currently a full-time student pursuing a master's degree in psychological counseling, he is conducting research on fathers of children with disabilities. After completing his master's degree, Bob hopes to continue his work in a Ph.D. program.

Matrix

Nicholas Kappes

Birth

Andrew was born into an unconventional family characterized by adventure, creativity, and independence. My wife, Linda, is an only child. I have enjoyed my two brothers. We wanted another child to love, and thought it would be good for William, our 5-year-old, to have company.

Linda had a tough pregnancy—nausea for months. A routine test revealed a problem with her alpha-fetoprotein level. The doctor was not especially alarmed but we were referred to a genetic counselor, who crisply described our odds and options. Linda and I agreed to give birth—to a red brick if necessary—rather than take a life from the womb. The odds were so slim—1 in 100 chances—for a birth defect. The low alpha-fetoprotein level could easily have been a fluke.

During a third-trimester ice storm Linda was hospitalized with a vicious flu and a 104° fever. I worried feverishly about Linda and the baby "overcooking." Happily, she came home in a few days. Having a lot to do, we went on with our pregnancy, forgetting genetic concerns and preparing enthusiastically. When it was his time, Andy came so quickly that police stopped us for doing 75 on the way to the hospital!

Andrew was beautiful. He looked like the baby Buddha! But the delivery room nurses didn't share my excitement. They were busy relieving his blocked airway, working very hard to get him to cry. He was incredibly relaxed—almost "rubbery"—in sharp contrast to most tight, screeching, red-faced newborns. I was profoundly moved by his calmness—he looked so wise!

Nine hours later, as we reveled joyfully with our beautiful newborn, the pediatrician appeared in our hospital room and tersely informed us that Andy had Down syndrome—Trisomy 21—a third chromosome 21 in *every* cell of his body. According to the doctor, Andy wasn't "terribly affected," but manifested diagnostic criteria, such as low muscle tone. Chromosomal testing would confirm Down Syndrome.

I had been alive 46 years and this was my worst moment. Words are inadequate to describe this emotional cross-current: the peak of joy at the birth of my fine new son and the devastation at the death of my expectations. Moving back and forth between the extremes of emotional continuum *within the same second* is an experience reserved for few—fortunately. This powerful emotional oscillation between positive and negative emotions persists to this day—now slowly fading, like the earsplitting reverberation of a giant bell heard dangerously close. This was the perfect karmic kickback for an arrogant man who had always seen the retarded as the butts of a lifetime of MR jokes. I cried—perhaps screamed—I can't remember.

From that moment on, my greatest challenge has been to control my fear of the unknown—its chilling effects so powerfully employed by writers of horror tales. Ignorance isn't bliss—it can be devastating; pure hell. Usually, our creative imagination is our most powerful ally—but, in a dearth of information imagination ravages us like a hungry beast. Perversely, fear's monster gorges itself on *lack* of information. When not knowing exactly what is meant by a diagnosis or disease, condition or syndrome, our *negative* creative powers become unchecked, and our imagination will fill the gap with its own horrors.

For the first year I didn't sleep more than an hour at a time, waking to make sure that Andy would not slip away into SIDS. Listening to his breathing, I spent long dark vigils encountering my own worst demons and agonizing about a grim future. What would he look like? What would his life be like? I knew more about the backside of the moon and the bottom of the sea than about people with Down syndrome. My wretched imagination supplied me with the worst. The restless nights and my grim fantasies were a frightening—if unavoidable—waste.

(Now, almost six years later, at least I worry about *realities*—but I still never sleep more than three hours without waking up.)

Fortunately, Andrew has one of the finest mothers on earth. Gifted with the inner strength of an Italian, English, Canadian Indian, and German ancestry, she resolutely applies her fine intelligence and undampened spirit in pursuit of the best for him. Her role requires keen awareness and foresight, the strongest will, unwavering faith in Andy's potential, and the patience of Job and Florence Nightingale combined. She fills the bill magnificently. Linda's steady strength helped me keep my sanity and perspective in many tight spots. And there are many more tight spots to come. He couldn't have a better mom.

The toughest role is reserved for Andy's older brother by five years—William. For a Calvin-and-Hobbes-type kid to suffer the enormous refocus of the family and endure long-term hair-trigger tension is incredibly unfair. Andy, now almost six, is mostly non-verbal, and he needs an extraordinary amount of vigilance and "watching." He doesn't participate in the "appropriate-brother-play" thing often. It will continue to be a major challenge to get William into adulthood without the impression that he has been given a raw deal. And he must be prepared for the role of legal guardianship when we pass away. At an early age, William is being forced to learn that life isn't fair. Fortunately, he is very intelligent, good-natured, resourceful, and generous.

Struggle

Andy is strong, tall, and slender with beautiful almond-shaped blue eyes and blond hair. He has a gorgeous full-mouthed pointy-chinned smile. We call him "Hutley"—as in hut-2–3–4, hut-2–3–4, hut-2–3–4—like a military march. Hutley never stops. Even when calmly eating his toast (always butter side down), his feet barely slow down. Down syndrome is usually characterized by lack of enthusiastic gross motor activity, so we were delighted by Hutley's vigorous energy output! He was the exception—always moving. After several years it became apparent that he couldn't *remain still!*

With little interest in the little things of life (much preferring "the Big Picture"), Andy cannot be induced to play with small toys—or many toys at all. Although books do not interest him, he loves music, and plays his collection of keyboards. Stopping long enough to focus on anything is life's hardest challenge for him.

While watching Barney, Andy stands and twirls a sock or karate belt freshly stolen from his brother's room. He will spin himself round and round for 30 minutes then suddenly shoot off like a rocket at full speed, without displaying a trace of dizziness. His incessant, self-stimulating behavior is called "perseveration." As a baby, when placed on his tummy, he would wave his hands back and forth in rays of sunlight for hours—casting an oscillating shadow onto the carpet inches from his nose. We are told that he needs this constant visual and vestibular (balance/movement) stimulation to remain alert and aware—an unending, heroic struggle for him. Sometimes, I see him struggling to escape his condition.

Andy is a "runner," with a sixth sense about open doors and ways out of wherever. He takes off with a flash and never looks back. At the zoo he "escaped" and ran for two hours as I followed him. We admire his sense of self-security—and live in horror of his potential escape. We have complex gate locks and heavily greased kid-safe doorknobs in a dedicated effort to prevent disaster. Twice he *has* escaped, but a lucky catch by an alert neighbor brought him back to us. Still, he gets smarter and stronger every day!

Hutley forces us to march along with him to the endless drumbeat of his cavalcade of appointments, visitations, and therapy sessions. And we march to meetings of parent support groups, disability organizations, and agencies. This engulfing maelstrom of activity absorbs our energy, time, and money—all in pursuit of the Holy Grail of Repair—which will "fix" Hutley or fix society enough to enable him to lead a happy and productive life.

Fortunately, we didn't receive Hutley's "Triple-Plus Diagnosis" until he was four and a half. Pervasive Developmental Disorder was the buzzword used when he didn't fit "normal Downs developmental" criteria. Now that he is going on 6, he manifests some autistic be-haviors—difficulty forming relationships, frequently avoiding eye contact, and sometimes being emotionally inaccessible. He is unable to focus, manifesting some "At-tention Deficit/Hyperactive Disorder" criteria as well. In spite of continuous therapy, his infrequent speech is apraxic. His lack of speech progress is very painful for us—but more painful for him. However, he has become an excellent cash cow for the therapy industry.

If I pick Andy up he will look away—putting his cheek close to mine while gripping my chin with his hand—a greeting custom, no doubt, from Planet X! I didn't get my first kiss until he was 5. He teases us with occasional "normal" days—with eye contact, engage-ment, and speech efforts—maybe a rare kiss! However, once he says words, we are not likely to *ever* hear them again! (As an armchair anthropologist and science fiction buff, I always dreamed of making contact with an alien civilization. I have my *own* inscrutable and adorable alien now!) In spite of his "Triple-Plus Diagnosis," we feel blessed. Andy is an incredible and remarkable human being: truly unique, dauntingly complex, humorous, and fleetingly engaging—self-contained and intelligent in wholly unique ways. Besides, he is really cute.

His disabilities reflect the truth that we are all disabled, and viewed as such by those fully enabled and competent in a particular field that we aren't—football, mathematics, art, sailing, hard rock climbing. In many cases we can, through hard work and study, eventually attain competence. But there are many things we can *never* become proficient in. We let these things go, refocusing on the things we *can* do. We are forced both by choice and personal limitation to select endeavors that fit us; endeavors that we can succeed in and have fun doing.

Many fields of possibility are closed to Andy. I don't see him becoming a chemist or a race car driver (although he might want to). His field of choice has been narrowed—but from his *relative* point of view I think he will be drawn to those life pursuits that attract him, and for which he is equipped—just like the rest of us. Our choices are narrowed too—whether by class, education, accidents of birth with respect to geography, race, economic station, the nature of the economy, revolution, war, and weather. We all must encounter, endure, and overcome frustration. Andy has struggled, and will continue to struggle—just like the rest of us.

Pain

At the beginning, there was intense grief over the loss of expectations that are the foundation of enthusiastic parenthood. Closely held in the hearts of moms and dads are images of an ideal family and successful, happy children who bring us bliss in our old age. With a disabil-

ity, this story-book of family life cracks. Letting go of expectations about a child's future is agonizing—but it is
only one facet of the trauma caused by a child's disability.

Sometimes I am overwhelmed by successive waves
of fear, anxiety, and frustration. Career work becomes
impossible. Time freezes—then jerks forward. Struggles
with Andy's developmental milestones—the constant
seeking, arranging, and applying of myriad therapies,
combined with the actual minute-to-minute management
of a son who is marginally autistic and mentally retarded—push me beyond the breaking point. I struggle,
accommodate, bend, and finally break—eventually healing in a new, but reduced, broken form. It is terribly
hard to remain focused on my dreams and goals.

How far from my life dreams will I have to devi-
ate? I suspect inconceivably far. I fear that my life—
planned and fantasized about in my teens and 20's, built
in my 30's, being shaped in my 40's—being readied for
the grand enjoyment and fulfillment of the 50's, 60's,
and, hopefully, beyond, will be ripped away by over-
whelming preoccupation with the demanding realities of
raising a child with significant disability. There is an abys-
mal feeling of this deep despair and loss of direction—
how will I cope with all of this, and how will I ever
fulfill my pre-disability dreams and goals?

Even more subtle is the dreadful loss of creative im-
petus. For some families this may not be a problem, but
for us it has been devastating, as we have both been self-
employed in artistic professions for decades. Creative
ideas need time and space in which to develop—ideas occur spontaneously, but must be squeezed into a "practical reality" by means of hard work and focused

attention. With pluck and luck one might eventually realize a decent return from a good idea.

Now, unrelenting stress constantly side-tracks us, draining our time and energy. Most creative ideas and projects stall. It has been difficult and demanding to bring Andy just *this* far. Long-term financial consequences to this "Loss of Great Ideas" are too scary to calculate, but now I understand why when disability is forced on families by accident or negligence, the awards can be in the millions.

Another, more insidious aspect is the gradual realization that we are in the grip of a psychological python that inexorably squeezes time, energy, creative and financial resources out of us. While another family is anxiously trying to choose and pay for a cute little boat or a fun little vacation, we find ourselves desperately trying to locate and pay for appropriate physical and speech therapies, sometimes spending our resources on unproven, but expensive "fringy" therapies. We try our best to have a normal life—but in the long run it is utterly inescapable that over the years we will pour our time and energy, emotional, psychological, and financial resources into helping Andy.

Often it seems that the universe has turned inside out! Planet X has invaded our cozy solar system, establishing a new planetary order. Parent careers and plans are no longer the sun at the center, with the "kid planets" orbiting around at various distances. Hutley has become the new center of gravitation around which all must orbit. Space and time have collapsed. The distances from this new sun to the planets have decreased, speeding up planet rotational speed and orbital velocity. The days and the years have shrunk, but are more densely packed with responsibility.

Plans and decisions, jobs and career possibilities, educational opportunities and potential home locations—from counties to countries—are weighed in terms of their compatibility with "Andy's situation." Many, many dreams go out the window—some immediately—others die slowly in the dawn of new realizations. Schools and therapists, even cities and states—because of their programs, services, and attitudes—become addictive lifelines that cannot be broken or substituted. All life plans for everyone must be evaluated in the light of his needs. Even decades from now his brother's future family will not be free to live far from Andrew.

Disability can create the appearance of family dysfunctionality. Drained by duties and depression—a family implodes and isolates itself. Sometimes it is like being a family of gophers—we incessantly dig our own tunnel, only occasionally having time to pop out to see other gophers, who, like us, are equally busy! Old friends become uncomfortable and gradually drift away. People in general want a positive life and see disability as a difficult struggle that they would rather not watch. Others discriminate and avoid us—some people still believe that their children can "catch" retardation.

To have a child with a disability is to realize that no family has a storybook life. All children tax their parents to the core of their being, try them by fire, and break their hearts repeatedly. Loss and separation, accident and disease, family trauma, failed plans, and even success can have painful consequences.

Growth

Besides financial rewards and creative fulfillment, adventure and the pleasures of friendship, there are other aspects of life to develop. Though it has been very painful, I've realized personal growth by trying to transcend my own selfish interests. Simply conquering prejudice about citizens suffering with mental disability represents a complete about-face for me. I have been indelibly sensitized to the misfortunate in our society. I have developed far greater compassion. This is part of a life-long journey—I would not have come this far if Andy hadn't come into my life. And the seeds of a good man are already sown into the soul of Andy's brother.

Though far from perfect, our society has gone to great lengths to help people with disabilities. There are many helpful programs, agencies, groups, and dedicated professionals. Many have dedicated themselves to self-less social service. There is an enormous, but barely visible, infrastructure of volunteerism and philanthropy. A greater sense of social responsibility has impelled me to join several organizations that serve the interests of the disability community. These commitments further exacerbate my feelings of over-commitment! However, there are great satisfactions in knowing that I am doing *something* to help.

I am humbled by the dignity and strength with which other families bear the weight of their disability—some burdened with inconceivably dreadful situations. I am astonished that the depth of disability can exceed my capacity to imagine—yet each day these families sacrifice and struggle to create a fulfilling and dignified life for these children and their siblings. These are incredibly gritty, courageous struggles, and there are many unsung heroes.

The greatest measure of our humanity is how we accept and care for those unable to care for themselves. This is the cornerstone in the foundation of our human civilization—placed on the bedrock that separates us from most members of the animal kingdom. In the end, most of us become *very* disabled—the most powerful athletes, the brightest scientists, the noisiest politicians, the most beautiful actors, the richest investors, and the wildest adventurers. Old age and infirmity reduce most of us to a helpless condition before death calls. I firmly believe that those who have dealt generously with disability will find it easier to accept this stage in life when their turn comes!

The rain comes, plums ripen, leaves turn, and snow falls. Through these seasons my sons grow toward their future no more certain than my own. Nothing in life is assured for the good or bad, beautiful or ugly, sharp or dull citizen. We all must take our place at the roulette wheel of life. Some things work out, and some things do not. And we are all disabled and struggling. Those who do not believe this are simply out of touch with themselves. Beneath the veneer of successful personalities and prominent families we always find sorrow and suffering, disappointment and struggle. Struggle characterizes life itself—without it growth would be impossible.

Disability does not present itself without a set of gifts. I derive comfort from the thought that it's the sand grain that seeds the oyster's pearl...and pearls are rare among oysters! The child with a disability enables—perhaps forces—the family to grow layers of unconditional love, selfless consideration, and quiet strength around this unusual person. Peering into the crib of a child with disability in the predawn moonlight can bring tears of truly unconditional love—love that will not be based on report card performance, scores as a star quarterback, or excellent performance as a respected trial lawyer. This love is for who this person *is,* for their qualities, their trials and for the inner strength they must develop to take their place. It is their struggle—we can only hope and help, watch and love.

Faith

What is intelligence to be used for? To build, to enjoy life, to question, to scheme, to control? Just why are most of us so smart? Is it necessary to be very intelligent to have a good time being alive? Most intelligence seems to be used "offensively"—taking advantage of situations or people to create profit or control others. How much intelligence goes into appreciating a sunrise, the autumn leaves, a kitten at play, or fine music?

IQ has measured all of us—yet we know how remarkably little IQ has to do with beingness. And there must be many types of IQ—at least art and design, mathematical, linguistic, interpersonal, manual, theatrical, athletic, political, and moral. The matrix of evaluation metrics applied to children is not as large as the children themselves are—it's impossible to be guided by IQ alone when reflecting upon these people's inner experiences and ability.

I find myself wondering how it is to be mentally retarded on a second-to-second basis. How is it different—and yet similar—to those of us "fully enabled?" What do those of us who are fully enabled do with our consciousness most of the time? What do people with mental retardation think about? What does the world look like to them? Is their perception of their local universe fuzzy and dulled? Do things not make sense? Is intelligence to be used for interpreting sense experience of the world—classifying the colors and fine structures of the plants in the world garden? Is it for creating a sense of self as a separate entity in the world of other separate entities? Is it for debating such questions as "What is intelligence for?" Is it a portal to godliness?

Andy doesn't seem to inhabit the same plane of existence as we do. More accurately, his plane is more different from the normal differences separating most of the rest of our realities. When I see Andy excitedly looking out the window at the branches moving in the wind, when he responds to fine jazz and classical music, and when he smiles as we speed through the forest on a sunny day, I see him living his human experience just as fully—perhaps more fully—than anyone else I know. He does not have the capability to give me detailed abstract reports about his experiences, but he sure as hell *lives* to the hilt!

I think Andy and the Buddha may have lots in common—Andy is mostly "Being Here Now." He seems to be focused on the present with an intensity and relish that are inspiring. He never looks bored. He does not do much pondering; he absorbs reality and unifies with it to a remarkable degree—sometimes I believe he "becomes grass"—"becomes our family dog"—"becomes the leaves and branches of the tree," rather than *thinking* about these things. I think his consciousness is pure and unaffected by the steady bombardment of negativity that is damaging the rest of us. He seems to live unfettered with reflective thought and ego—he simply *is*—and he enjoys *being*.

The citizen with mental retardation or disability might find the proverbs "Water seeks its own level" and "Birds of a feather flock together" as true today as when observed by Lao-Tzu in 580 BC. Indeed, these folks group, form companionship and consensus, and share with each other the joys and satisfactions in their challenges and accomplishments. Inclusion in society at large is necessary and wonderful, but it does not remove individual difference—it may underscore it—deepening their need to be with peers who truly empathize with their unique "spot."

In our darkest reflections of the future we project our fears, sensitivities, and personal inadequacies onto these special children; we imagine their future struggles and rejections and dread their awful potential loneliness. But projection is dangerous—it sells them short on their ability to find their *own* level and their *own* birds. They will develop their own interests. They will discover their own friendships—just as we have. They will experience rejection—just as we have. They will have lonely boring days—just as we have. And they will fabricate an engaging reality—just as we have.

I find peace in relativity. It governs our universe—it also governs our lives. No matter who or where we are we can always look up to greater and down to lower. Presidents and kings have their heroes and their inadequacies. No one is completely happy or has it all figured out to their satisfaction, and even those in tragic, painful circumstances cling to each precious moment of life—so it must be worth it for all.

I've never met a person who thought life was easy! Should we feel sorry for our children with disability? No one can convince me that I should not—I already feel sorrow for the whole lot of humanity—presidents and popes included! Andy will suffer like the rest of us—but he *will* be OK.

Nicholas Kappes was born in 1943 and grew up in Cincinnati, Ohio. Chemistry and geology, art and archeology have characterized his lifetime fascination with form and structure, symmetry and time. He moved to Los Angeles in 1963 to live out his engineering career fantasies. In 1971, he began his "art life" as a photographer, which lasted 23 years. In 1984, Nick and his wife, Linda, escaped to Seattle and began their family, which now includes two fine sons. Following a resolution of a mid-life crisis in 1993, he turned to the "concrete reality" as designer/fabricator working in metal and stone. He struggles to finish his book Get Control of Your Art Career Now! *and remains a closet archaeologist. He is an advocate for the disability community.*

The Hardest Lesson: Learning to Accept

Lloyd W. Robertson

My daughter, Katie, was born in July of 1988. At age 5, she has become increasingly easy to care for, yet for me it is increasingly difficult to accept her life as it is. It is especially difficult to imagine it stretching on for years—into my wife's and my old age, or after our deaths. Laura admits to having sudden thoughts of what life would be like if Kate were normal, a big sister to Benjamin, who is three. The thought brings tears, and then the mood passes. More than Laura, I seem to be stuck, right at the beginning. The first step for parents like us, we have been told, is to mourn the healthy child who was not born, and welcome and nurture the damaged one who was. I wonder how anyone can accept the unacceptable.

Sometimes, I think my frustration and anger will overpower my love for Katie. Or I think that I should feel a more perfect love that can withstand everything. How could I not feel that I am letting her down? Yet I keep on learning, along with Laura, how to live with Kate. Accepting our life means learning the hardest lessons I have faced; but we are doing it, somehow.

Laura and I knew, practically at her birth, that Katie was severely brain damaged, but it took us a while to realize she was never going to develop intellectually or walk, talk, learn, or communicate beyond indicating discomfort. She experiences hypertonicity, spasticity, and seizures of various kinds. She does not smile (although she used to fleetingly, as she awoke in the morning); she generally presents to the world a face either of obvious discomfort or of impassive, Queen Victoria-like calm: "we are not amused." Her only diagnosis is "cerebellar displasia and severe psychomotor retardation," catch-all phrases, technically accurate, but not very revealing.

I say we came to realize these terrible facts, but many times we have been disappointed and even shocked by events that we knew were coming: a continual need for lung care and tons of medications, growth that prevents us from carrying her easily, a curving spine that will probably need a brace and/or surgery, and ironic birthdays. We realize facts about Kate, but we don't always accept them.

In the spring before her third birthday, Kate developed pulmonary edema as a complication of pneumonia, and nearly died. In some ways, it was a comedy of errors: nurses were coming and going at our house, and we were on the phone with Kate's doctors discussing her symptoms and what we should do. We had reached a point where the doctors trusted our judgment, partly because they knew we would seek good advice. We were hesitant to take her to the big city hospital, an hour away, if she could be treated at home. No one caught the fact that Kate had pneumonia until a respiratory therapist—an occasional visitor who had known Kate since the early days—noticed the puffiness in her body and said "pulmonary edema." When we got to the city, the respiratory specialist looked at the X-ray, listened to Kate's breathing, and said something like: "Katie is very sick. If we give her a diuretic to help her pass the fluid in her body, she might survive the weekend; on the other hand, she might not." Once again, we had known such a thing could happen, and that it might be a blessing. We had even prepared papers to say DNR—"do not resuscitate"—if Kate came to a point of extreme illness; that's why she was not going on a ventilator. Yet we were plunged into shock and horror at what was happening.

We took her home and cared for her as best we could. Everyone we spoke to—including, again, Kate's wonderful doctors on the phone—was very compassionate. I think what I felt overall during crises like this was a kind of hyper-sensitivity, as though my senses were extra acute, and I could hear small sounds at great distances, or at least I could respond to Katie wherever she was. My skin felt as though it was stretched tight; I could not breathe deeply with my chest cavity so constricted. On the whole this was uncomfortable, like being squeezed into a space that was too tight, but it also brought a sense of seeing deeply into things, or being able to learn quickly and make decisions. Katie survived, and we had mixed feelings then—or at least I did—just as we did through the whole trauma.

Katie's life had lasted nearly three long years. Some people, medical and otherwise, had suggested during her first year or two that she might not live long with such massive handicaps, and especially with her erratic breathing, which had required major surgery and still requires nursing care for her lungs. Others, more realistic as it turned out, had tried to suggest that we should prepare for Kate to have a long life, so that we could make plans and consider implications. When we realized that our ordeal might go on for years, that what we had just endured was only one more crisis, we felt completely burned out. We had asked before about places where Katie might live outside our home, and had even toured a state-run facility, but we did not think there was any place that would provide the care she needed. Now, in desperation, we asked a social worker if there were any more options available. There was a new children's unit in a nursing home that we could look at; within a few months, after some trial periods, she was living there.

Telling the story this way makes it seem that we considered mainly our own feelings and convenience, and we didn't think enough about Kate. We can say we waited until we found just the right place, with a nursing staff trained in pediatrics, all hands-on care done by nurses instead of aides, and a low ratio of staff to patients; we can say we visited twice or three times a week, usually for hours at a time, but it still might be true that we were overwhelmed with grief. We thought we needed to have some time with Benjamin, whose young life had been dominated by his sister's problems. Now we think he can benefit from growing up with her, and it would do him no favor to have a sibling living "away" somewhere. It's hard to say who has final wisdom on such matters, or where to turn for such wisdom. What I am trying to show is that we have struggled to achieve acceptance, and even a kind of peace, and I am still struggling.

After eighteen months, the State closed down the children's unit where Kate was living. We could see that the thinking behind this action was well-intentioned: "institutions" had consistently left children out of sight and out of mind. At best, as a rule, children were not stimulated to ensure they developed as fully as possible; at worst they suffered neglect and abuse, as many people in nursing homes do. Thus progressive thinking is against a child living anywhere other than at home, and we were made to feel like followers of Hitler for wanting to keep Katie where she was. Laura made hundreds of phone calls to get everything set up at home again: funding from private insurance and from the state; supplies for respiratory equipment and tube feedings; medications; diapers. And Katie came home, by this time approaching her fifth birthday.

Now we've gone through a move, involving a six-day drive, and we have less help in Canada than we did in Minnesota. Despite everything, Laura is pleased, now, to have Kate at home. The main thing, she says, is that Katie obviously likes her routine with us; she seems comfortable and responsive. She goes to kindergarten for half-days, and she seems to respond in some vague but positive way to the other children talking to her and playing with her. We noticed the same thing in a daycare in Minnesota, after she came home.

Benjamin goes through periods of ignoring her, but usually makes a point of climbing on her chair or bed to kiss her once a day, and Katie responds to him as much as to anyone. Sometimes he tries to get her to grab a toy, or at least reach out to it, but she has never gripped anything, and her limited reaching seems to be more to remove discomfort, especially around her tracheostomy tube, than for something pleasant or positive. Ben has had problems determining whether Katie is really playing with him or not. I suppose he always will.

We don't know what it is like to be Katie, or how things seem to her. She can communicate by grimacing, in extreme cases by crying (soundlessly because of her trach, which has been made permanent), by "huffing and puffing," and by twisting her body to find a new position (although she cannot turn herself). It has always been harder to see any joy or pleasure in her responses, although to those of us who know her, there are degrees of mellowness and relaxation which can suggest enjoyment. When these moods or responses are combined with a kind of wide-eyed attempt to get a glimpse of something, anything, they remind us of a curious child enjoying some stimulation. She will sometimes turn toward a sound, and in general she responds to our voices. But except for startling at loud noises, she does not show any truly consistent response. Does the effort get to be too much? Or do her senses come and go on her, giving her glimpses of confusing images, snatches of tantalizing sounds (as another diagnosis, "cortical blindness," suggests)? We simply don't know. Laura says she can tell the difference between when Kate is totally blind and when she is not. She was unbelievably uncomfortable when she was little, and her EEG shows almost constant seizure activity. We fear that she suffers periodic jolts of neurological activity that stop her from responding (and would probably render any of us shaky if not insane) much like the deafening noises inflicted on intelligent people to keep them from thinking in Kurt Vonnegut's story "Harrison Bergeron."

I am glad to see Katie more comfortable than ever, sleeping through the night, having a semblance of a normal life. But I am frustrated at the limitations on our present life, and I fear for the future. Beginning about the time we knew we had to bring Kate home again, I have found my characteristic mood to be one of restless anxiety, slipping and sliding into rage. As I look back, I think the arrangement while Katie was in the nursing home was nearly perfect. The reason, frankly, is that I had far less anxiety about her when I was not actually with her; it all seemed manageable. Now, with her home with us, it can all seem unmanageable. It does not help that my career, and hence my ability to support the family, including Katie's unique and expensive needs, is in doubt. It took me a long time to finish my Ph.D., and I now compete for entry-level positions with people who are younger, and who often have credentials that are more in demand. Every spring I am forced to wonder whether I will have a job the following fall, and the falls after that. All I have had, so far, are temporary replacement positions. It somehow seems fitting that when we moved back to Canada, where we are citizens, we discovered the recession had been worse than in the U.S., and it would be difficult for either of us to get a job of any kind.

Of course I know that similar and worse difficulties are handled cheerfully by many people. Indeed, I have sometimes been more cheerful myself, even when things were arguably worse. Kate's first year was unbelievably difficult, yet in hindsight at least, we were too busy to

think a lot about it, we were quick to laugh (sometimes
hysterically), and we kept thinking that Kate's life would
not be all bad news—something exciting and hopeful
could happen. This strange hopefulness resulted partly
from spending a lot of time in a modern children's hospital. I could not have imagined such a place if I had not
seen it in some detail. Katie spent one night in newborn
intensive care—special smocks for visitors; tiny patients
in space-age incubators (an old, cozy word) called
"isolettes" (a rather creepy word); wires, IV tubes, and
machines; bright fluorescent lights, luminescent dials,
tiny blinking lights, and sometimes semi-darkness for the
babies, and the beeping noises of alarms going off—almost always false alarms. We were given our first definite bad news about Kate in this place. Later we had
more and more bad news, a long stay in a regular ward
where the quality of nursing varied quite a bit (some
nurses superb, others floored by some of Katie's needs)
and some surgeries. As long as your child is in such a
place, and doctors speak as though there is still some
high-tech magic that might be tried, it is difficult not to
have hope.

Modern medicine sometimes prolongs miserable
lives, and surely it generally contributes to our excessive
concern for our bodies, and for a life measured by its
length. Yet, there are many cases now in which doctors
undeniably effect cures, and treatments that make noticeable improvements in people's lives. As a parent, to feel
there is hope for one's child can make the most miserable situation acceptable. To have that hope ended,
while others are getting cured, is to taste bitter despair.
Unless you have a belief in the eternal that gives you
some perspective, you can easily think hospitals are the

temples of our age, manipulating our deepest hopes and fears and dividing us into those who can be helped, and those who cannot. Laura and I both reached the point where we didn't want Katie to spend the night in hospital—it was simply more worry for us—but a visit to the doctors, a change in medications, or an adjustment to her chair, could cheer us up. Something could be done; something could get better. Having her at home makes me think nothing of importance will change, except perhaps for the worse—that surgery she may need on her spine, for example.

More matter-of-factly, I may have stayed more cheerful about Kate when I was busier with her cares and needs. There is a helpful cliché here that perhaps fathers should think about more: standing nearby and watching your child with disabilities struggle and be cared for is more heartbreaking than pitching in and doing at least some of what needs to be done. On the other hand, I have the problem of being pulled in more than one direction because of family and career, whereas Laura has not worked full-time since before Kate was born. Whichever I spend a lot of effort on, work or family and Kate, I usually feel I am neglecting something important. I have an impression, based partly on conversations of parents of children with handicaps, that fathers are more likely to feel anger, while mothers are more likely to feel sadness. Maybe this is not so much a natural difference, as it is a reflection of the fact that men are still likely to be the primary wage-earners—responsible for financial security, now and in the future, and thus likely to panic at the thought of a chronically handicapped child whose care is very expensive, and who is likely to outlive his or her parents.

Peter DeVries wrote a beautiful and blood-curdling book called *The Blood of the Lamb,* about a series of deaths close to the protagonist, culminating in the story of his daughter dying of leukemia. He expresses plenty of rage himself, and meets another father in the hospital who insists on being theological. To anyone who will listen he says things like: "How could a God let this happen, *cause* this to happen? Prove to me that there's a God and then I'll *really* despair!"

I was in a group with a father whose child has spina bifida; whenever the people he worked with heard about another surgery, they would express the hope that this would "do it," even though he had explained repeatedly that there was a lifetime of procedures and hospital visits ahead. What really drove him up the wall was his co-worker's pious encouragement: "You know, God wouldn't have given you this special challenge unless He knew you could handle it." "What do we have," asked this dad, almost in Yiddish fashion, "signs on our chests saying 'pick us'?"

Perhaps the real problem is that I am pushing 40, and the various frustrations in my life, including Kate's struggles, have brought me a mid-life crisis a bit early. I miss a sense of compensation, especially when it comes to Kate. It is difficult to say: I may have given up x, but at least I have y. I have accumulated partial victories in fields where only complete victories count. My experiences have been instructive without making me wise, and have put me in touch with eternal questions without helping me see God. My life is unfortunate but not tragic; I am enraged but not heroic.

I recently read an article on the "realist" paintings of Alex Colville. All his works suggest something beautiful and natural which ought to be restful and comforting: horses; people in the nude, relaxing in the sun; people and animals comfortable together. Yet they all convey a sense of impending menace, as is obvious in his well-known *Horse and Train*. We have discovered that menace, too, that vulnerability: our tenuous balance can be shattered.

Like Bill Murray's character in *Groundhog Day*, it is easy to fall into a spell, having to live identical days (or nearly identical), irritated with the routine, anxious about the passing of time and advancing mortality, and thus more and more irritable. I am forced to see that this only makes things worse and makes the already long day even longer. I think I have stumbled on the same "secret" way out that Murray's character used. Only I'm having trouble making use of my knowledge.

The resolution of *Groundhog Day* is oddly similar to *Beauty and the Beast*: the spell cannot be broken until the hero truly loves another human being at least as much as he loves himself. Perhaps this is how we are supposed to give up—or at least modify—male fantasies like the warrior in the *Iliad* and the wanderer in the *Odyssey*. In my case, I must love my daughter Kate enough to want her to go on living, and be comfortable, no matter what sacrifice this requires of me.

As Laura reads these words, she reminds me that this is only the gloomy side of life, and I have other moods. I can't be expected to accept and enjoy Kate exactly as if she were normal, and I shouldn't blame myself for not doing so. The stale cliché is true: I have to accept the limitations on Kate's life as best I can. It helps to see that life is worth living, and has its moments of sweetness. Laura enjoys cuddling with Kate, and says it feels

like she still has a baby. Ben likes to see if Kate will turn
her head one way or the other, or open her eyes, and he
will laugh at her. I have my own part in these joys, and I
mustn't let fears about the future spoil them.

---

*Lloyd W. Robertson was born in Drumheller, Alberta,
and attended University of Alberta, Brock University and
the University of Toronto, where he was awarded a Ph.D.
in political science. He has taught at Brock University in
St. Catherine's, Ontario, and St. Olaf College and Carle-
ton College in Northfield, Minnesota. He currently
teaches at St. Thomas University in Fredericton, New
Brunswick. Earlier non-academic pursuits include playing
keyboards for a wedding and party band and work as a research assistant for the Alberta Legislature and the House
of Commons in Ottawa. He reads during every spare moment and enjoys movies. Married in 1978, Lloyd and his
wife, Laura, have two children.*

A New Calling

Stanley Reiff, Sr.

My family and I love our new home in Kodiak,
Alaska. We recently moved here from North Pole,
Alaska—near Fairbanks—where we had lived for over
seven years. North Pole's long and severe winters were
taking a toll on our family, especially on our oldest son,
Stanley Jr. Stanley has cerebral palsy and uses a wheelchair. It was time to move. This move is just the latest
step in a long journey, a journey that six years ago
changed direction and took on a special significance.

I am a third-generation missionary. My grandparents were missionaries in Central America for almost 30
years. My parents were missionaries, and I was born and
raised overseas as a missionary kid. All my life I had
dreamed of continuing this heritage.

After I earned a college degree in religious education, my wife, Amy, and I moved to Alaska with the intention of becoming missionaries. Young and full of
enthusiasm, we spent a year settling into Alaska's culture

and climate. It was our hope to relocate to a remote village. It was during this time that our first child, Stanley, was born—two months early. Because he had no apparent complications, we continued with our plans to move to a tiny village in the Alaskan Interior—remote, but still on the road system.

Despite our best plans and deepest desire to serve, this move was not to be. By fall of that year, it was apparent that Stanley had serious problems. On a trip to Seattle for surgery we were told that Stanley had cerebral palsy. The following month, as we were adjusting to this news, we learned that our son had a permanent visual impairment. We were devastated by the rapid turn of events. Our move to the remote village was canceled.

As a minister, I was confused and bewildered by all of this. As you might imagine, the intersection (or should I say collision?) of my call to missionary work and the diagnosis of my son's disability shook my faith in God. My occupation was on hold. I had a lot of questions that had no easy answers: How can God allow this to happen to me? Why didn't God heal Stanley through divine intervention? Why did God allow this to happen to me? After all, I was His "servant" and there is a worldwide shortage of missionaries.

It didn't make any sense.

I grappled with these questions. While neither blaming or resenting Stanley, I struggled with what this event meant to my vocation as a missionary. If I was a plumber or an accountant, I may have been able to separate my job from my family and my personal pain. But as a minister, I could not separate my job from my faith. My faith is an integral part of my work.

Time, I am happy to report, has brought healing. I came to believe that either God is in control, or He is not God at all. I found great peace when I acknowledged that God indeed knew what was happening in our lives and that He would continue to provide guidance. Although I certainly did not know this then, Stanley would have a huge impact on my ministry. His life introduced me to a part of society I had not known or understood—families of children with special needs.

For a while, I left the ministry. Stanley's medical expenses were enormous and the ministry's health benefits were insufficient. I went to work for Alaska's Department of Fish and Game, which provided health benefits we desperately needed. As much as I liked the work, I felt somewhat unfulfilled. I still had a desire to return to full-time ministry. And that is what brought us all to Kodiak.

In Kodiak, I had been offered a paid ministry position. Kodiak also offered Stanley a warmer climate and the opportunity to be included in a regular education program. I worried about the uncertainties: Would he/we be accepted in this new community? Would we find the support services we need? The thought of moving from Fairbanks (with a population of 75,000) to Kodiak Island (with a total population of 15,000) was unnerving. Would the island have competent, compassionate therapists with good kid skills? Would he survive in a traditional classroom after being in a self-contained classroom with an outstanding teacher who cared deeply for him? What would his classmates say? Think? Do? We had worked closely with a fantastic team of pediatricians in Fairbanks. What medical support would we find

on this North Pacific island? Could we find a church
that would lovingly accept Stanley for who he is?

As it turns out, worrying was a waste of time. Stanley has adapted far better that we could have dreamed
and has made great strides in many areas. Since moving
here, Stanley has gone horseback riding, swimming, and
fishing. Stanley loves to fish, and Kodiak is a fisherman's
paradise! His therapists are wonderful, caring and sensitive to the needs of all the members of Stanley's family.
Despite my reservations, full inclusion at school has been
a dream come true. He enjoys a class full of peers who
interact with him constantly. When we are out shopping
we frequently meet many of his friends, who happily approach Stanley and visit with him. I have longed for the
day when Stanley would be included in the normal activities of childhood. Seeing this, I am fulfilled.

I realize that I am a hopeless, sentimental romantic.
I value family traditions and activities. I like Norman
Rockwell paintings. I find myself becoming teary-eyed at
weddings, especially at the songs about how the little
boy grows up so fast and is now getting married, and the
little girl grows up to be the wife of the groom's dreams.
It makes me wonder about Stanley's future: Will he be
privileged to experience a loving relationship with a wife
who loves him? Will he experience the joy of having children of his own? Will he achieve independence? I find
myself lying awake, thinking about these things.

(Right now, I would be content just to hear him
talk. I want to listen to what he has to say and learn of
his hopes, dreams, and ambitions. I really do miss that
part of our relationship.)

I think about Stanley's future almost daily. I am concerned about who will take care of him when he is an

adult. Where will he live? In a group home or maybe an apartment attached to our home? What about after I'm gone? Will his brothers and extended family love and care for him like Amy and I do? Who will provide for his needs? Who will respect his need for independence and individuality?

All my sons are quite young, but as the days roll on, I begin to wonder what the teenage years will be like. What will Stanley, Quinten, and Rhett's relationship be? Will they be close? Will they look after each other? What about dating? How will we deal with Stanley's sexuality? I don't know the answers, of course. I don't even know if these are the right questions! I take a small comfort in realizing that the concerns I have for Stanley's teenage years are really not that much different than the concerns I have for his brothers.

Sometimes I feel bad about the imbalance of time spent with my boys. I love all of them equally, but Stanley simply requires constant care: he must be fed, dressed, helped to use a toilet, rolled over during the night, and repositioned in his chair. I do special things with my other boys, but they just don't get the same amount of time. Will Quinten and Rhett resent Stanley because of this? They love Stanley now and help as much as a four- and two-year-old can—but will this change?

Recently, we've been on the roller coaster's downward slope. About three weeks ago, Amy got a call from school with a report that Stanley had a seizure—his first, except for a few he had when he was a month old. The next day, we had another call—another seizure. We are hoping that this is due to an electrolyte imbalance caused by flu-related dehydration. We still hope this is the cause even though his seizures started a week after he was over the flu. His doctors soon began talking about medical EEGs and seven-year medical interventions.

(Like so many other crises, this one is happening at Christmas time. Trips to the doctors, phone calls to physicians in Seattle and Fairbanks, all take time away from my other two boys. I can try to make up the time, but the time lost can never be regained. Where is the balance?)

Since this most recent crisis, I have had a hard time concentrating on work, this essay—anything. We were not comfortable with the doctors' recommendations—especially the seven-year medical treatment. Although his seizures may eventually require medical treatment, we decided to rely on our faith in God. We asked our minister and the church elders to pray for Stanley and for guidance. Following our time of prayer, we sensed a peace and calming of our unrest. Stanley has not had a seizure in over two weeks.

Christmas is a bittersweet time. We had a wonderful time, but I found my emotions as scattered as the snowflakes blowing outside my window. Finding an appropriate gift for Stanley is a challenge—I wish he could tell me what he really wants. However, I think we did well: a special therapy swing that he adores. His kicking legs, shrieks of laughter, and dancing eyes all tell me that he loves his new swing. But I still would love to hear him tell me, with his own words.

My son, it turns out, is quite a socialite. And like most socialites, Stanley loves the flurry of activities that accompany Christmas. I loved watching him as he passed out pecan pies to his teacher, therapists, atten-

dant, and principal just before Christmas. His eyes sparkled as he distributed the pies, and he would flash the
biggest grin. The recipients, of course, showered him
with attention and affection and Stanley continued to
glow.

We went caroling with our church, and Stanley reminded me of what Christmas is all about. As we stood
in the snow, singing, Stanley joined right in with his
shrieks of laughter and his attempts at singing. I must admit I am sometimes embarrassed when Stanley does this
in front of people we don't know. But on this night it
was all right. Like everyone else, Stanley was singing car-
ols and enjoying the snowy night's festivities. Who cares
what others think! Tonight we are celebrating Christmas!

With Christmas over and the new year approaching,
I find myself reflecting on the changes that have occurred in my life "since Stanley." In many ways, life with
a son who has a disability is a paradoxical event. It is frequently accompanied by an array of seemingly contradic-
tory emotions: profound happiness and satisfaction as
well as fear, sorrow, and suspense. In some ways, being a
father to Stanley has made profound changes in my lifestyle and thinking. On the other hand, it is not a whole
lot different than raising a child without disabilities.

As this essay attests, I have many questions, concerns, and misgivings, and probably will for many years
to come. Yet this experience has taught me, too. I hope I
am a more sensitive person: gentler in speech, slower to
cast judgment, and quicker to lend a helping hand or a
listening ear. I think more about my family's needs and
the time I need to spend with my sons. While I still have
serious workaholic tendencies, my families' needs come
before all other activities and responsibilities. I feel I

have a greater appreciation for this life, and a special appreciation for the life-to-come, when Stanley will run and jump and communicate and be understood by all. Although the events of the past six years have tested my faith, I am happy to report that I have passed the test! Family, friends, and support groups have been vital in coping with challenges posed by Stanley's special needs, but I have found my greatest source of strength to be my faith in God.

Stanley Reiff, Sr. was born in Jutiapa, Guatemala, to missionary parents. He lived in El Salvador and Guatemala until high school, when his family moved to south Florida. Stan completed college at the Hobe Sound Bible College with a double major in Ministerial Studies and Missionary Aviation. With his wife, Amy, Stan moved to Alaska, where they served as missionaries with Polar Evangelism. He cofounded Northwind Ministries, Inc., an organization devoted to transporting and providing support services to missionaries living in the Alaskan bush and has taught middle and high school English and social sciences. Stan is currently the Director of Finance and Development for the Kodiak Baptist Mission and serves as the President of the Board of Directors for PARENTS, Inc., a statewide organization serving parents of children with special needs.

Our Brave New World

———— ∞ ————

Ben Adams

I have three wonderful sons. My youngest is Caleb. He is an incredible example of love, happiness, determination, frustration, sadness, discrimination, and reality. As my wife, his two brothers, his grandmother, and his helpers struggle to teach Caleb how to behave appropriately in the real world, I often wonder why Caleb is the one who must change and why so little is expected of the real world. It's not that I don't expect Caleb to adapt and change, but I do dream of the day when society has overcome its prejudices and discomforts regarding people with disabilities.

When Caleb runs around the house, insisting that everyone be seated for dinner, or when he hears his mom's car come down the street and charges toward the garage, I am amazed at how sharp he is. For some reason, his significant attention deficit does not interfere with his ability to patiently watch someone manipulate a latch, lock, or other mechanical device. Quietly observing from a distance, Caleb will watch, focused and serious, until he has the action memorized. At 9 years, Caleb cannot read or write; however, he knows every lock in the house. With a wit as sharp as his eye, Caleb possesses a legendary sense of humor. He loves to call people "mom" or any other name besides their own. He laughs at his own jokes.

In nine years, Caleb has made such progress that it is hard to believe that when he was only four hours old, his pediatrician pulled me aside to pronounce: "You know Mr. Adams, some babies are just not meant to live. I'm recommending that you send Caleb to a medical facility better equipped to see exactly what is going on with your son. In the meantime, I think it best if you didn't say anything to your wife."

I was completely lost. What did he mean "some babies are just not meant to live?" What could I tell Renee? I ran into Renee's room and acted as if nothing was wrong. I had to be positive for Renee's sake! I lied and told her that I didn't know why they had not brought Caleb in to be with her. I needed to go home and see my family and my house. I needed to see something that was real and unchanged.

Seeing my family didn't help. With hopes hanging by thin threads, I tried to explain to my sister and her family that everything was OK. But soon I became very anxious. I ran down the street to the home of a pediatrician. "What did the doctor mean by pressure in the spinal fluid?" I asked him. I did not want to ask "How bad will it get?"

The pediatrician told me of a patient who had a shunt, a plastic tube that drained excess cerebral spinal fluid from her brain to her heart. As he explained this to me I was overcome with disbelief. I couldn't, I wouldn't believe that this could be happening to us. "It's amazing how well she is doing." he continued with a perplexed look on his face. He must have known that this was not what I wanted to hear.

I ran home to share this information with my family. As I tried to talk, I found that I couldn't—I could only cry.

During his first ten hours of life we learned that Caleb was born with hydrocephalus. As we would learn later, his hydrocephalus was caused by toxoplasmosis, an infectious disease harmful to developing fetuses. Over the next few days, the teams (it seemed that every specialty had its own team) of neurologists, neurosurgeons, infectious disease specialists, child development specialists, and neonatal pediatricians painted a dismal picture of what we could expect: a child confined to a crib, in need of multiple shunt revisions, with contractures, convulsions, and stuck at two-month developmental level.

I questioned the teams about the value of such a life. Must they do every possible thing to keep him going? I quickly learned that most doctors don't appreciate this line of inquiry. They have chosen this line of work to save lives.

The world as I knew it was no longer. I had no adequate way of processing this kind of information.

For some time before Caleb's birth, Renee and I had been associated with an organization that was a church, a club, and a cult. Members of this organization were taught to understand themselves and to become aware of

their intrapersonal needs and motivations. We were
taught to believe that one must take full responsibility
for every aspect of his or her life: before, during, and after. This group did not believe in accidents. They taught
that if you were self-directed, only good things would
happen to you.

So, what had we done wrong? Were we not believ-
ers? Did Caleb choose this life before he was born? Or
was it something simpler, but equally tragic? Had we se-
lected the wrong obstetrician? Should I have known that
cats can carry the toxoplasmosis microorganism? Again,
what had we done wrong? We—and our friends—struggled with the news. Renee and I would not believe that
we or Caleb had somehow chosen this way. Our so-
called circle of support interpreted this differently, however. They reaffirmed their belief that they, because of
their training and beliefs, had the power to bring only
good things to their lives.

When you don't believe in accidents or the random
nature of life, you are left to accept full responsibility for
everything that happens—good or bad. The pain caused
by our son's medical problems was immense. Had we
done this to him? Our feelings of guilt were tremendous.
Whenever we were with members of the group, our
son's problems would inevitably be discussed and de-
bated. The group's view was that "the self" chose this
for Caleb and us. Our view was that there are things in
life that no one can control. After a while, these debates
became exhausting and repetitive. We had to withdraw.
We felt very much alone during a time when we needed
so much support from our friends.

Making sense of a child's disability is different for
everyone. A person's background, baggage, and philoso-

phy will greatly determine how he interprets this event. Some religious beliefs acknowledge and even celebrate children with special needs. Most belief systems try to accommodate these children somehow. It was our misfortune to select a belief system that looked upon these children as a failure.

Unfortunately, most of us are guilty of searching for answers to questions such as "Why did this happen?" "Why did this happen to our child, my family, me?" "Have I won some perverted lottery?" "Could I have done something different that would have saved us all from this tragedy?"

I have learned that even *if* the cause of a child's disability is clearly someone else's fault, we are still liable to feel guilt. No matter who is at fault, the child is still affected and will be so for the rest of his or her life. No award in a malpractice suit will make the child better. If they serve any purpose, such awards can notify future practitioners to be careful and to pay attention.

Those of us who believe in an intelligence greater than our own can't help asking why such a being would allow such an event to happen. After I questioned why a "good" God would do this to an innocent child, one friend angrily answered, "Nobody said God is benevolent." Another said, "Well, he's not exactly a 'hands-on' God." Still another wondered whether it had to do with Caleb's karma. "Maybe Caleb did something in an earlier life." Another wondered if I had read the book of Job: "Maybe this is a test?" Yes, I thought: maybe this was to be a test of my ability to protect my family from an event that could cause pain and tragedy. Today, I feel it certainly *is* a test. I just wish I knew who was being tested and why.

Over the years, I've come to accept that the reason
for Caleb's disability has less to do with metaphysical reasons and more to do with sheer bad luck. Ours was an
unhappy combination of winning the perverted lottery
and having a sloppy obstetrician who, despite doing a
fine job with Caleb's older brother, failed to inquire
whether our family had a cat. Had we been asked, we
would have been told how cats can carry toxoplasmosis
and would have been much more careful.

Today, Caleb has developed far beyond the doctors'
grim prognoses. Despite the joy I feel for his many abilities, I must admit to lingering anger.

Soon after Caleb was born, I developed an adversar-
ial relationship with his doctors. This, I have found, can
easily happen when the needs and expectations of parents collide with those of professionals. The intensity of
the conflict can quickly escalate because the professionals are gatekeepers to all manner of things: medical care,
new procedures, educational services and settings, support, even hope.

I have been told by professionals that anger is part
of the process, a stage which *they* hope we will soon
move past. We receive the message that although there
will be disappointments that deserve anger, we must be a
reasonable, "professional" parent and appreciate that
everyone has good intentions. Despite its connection to
real-life issues, anger appears to have no place at meetings with service providers. Anger, I find, is especially un-
welcome at meetings (such as IEP conferences) where
the agenda is frequently predetermined by professionals.

The diagnosis of a child's disability will have profound impact on families. As a result of Caleb's disability, we have made new friends and find ourselves

constantly grappling with issues of education, social relations, and the future. Among the greatest concerns we find ourselves facing is that of stigma: stigma for the child with special needs and the stigma that families feel as well. Exclusion seems to be stigma's constant companion.

From the beginning, I have questioned why we exclude people with disabilities. Much of this exclusion is in the guise of "special" services: medical care is delivered by specialists; education is "special" and frequently delivered in "special" schools; activities are delivered in "special" recreation programs. When people with disabilities grow up, they can look forward to "special" work programs and "special" living situations.

As I search for reasons for this "special" paradigm, prejudice, stigma, and discrimination keep coming to mind. Even parents who favor institutional settings for their child frequently cite fear that society will not accept their child as their reason for placing him away from the community. In the community, they believe, their child will be stared at, rejected, or abused.

I understand their fears. I grew up on the "other side," feeling uncomfortable and afraid of people with disabilities. Despite this, I cannot accept the policy of forced segregation. It is, quite simply, wrong. There are no advantages—only disadvantages—to isolating such persons and their families. I know attitudes can be changed, and they must. I believe the first step is proximity. Over time, and with education, proximity brings understanding and acceptance.

Thus, I have come to believe that what is best for my son is education within a regular setting. Education that is stimulating and real in a setting that is practical and hopeful. Education with students who don't always have "appropriate behavior" but have real, typical behavior for Caleb to emulate. When people ask me why I believe he should be in a regular class, I explain that integration is a value I have for Caleb *and* his classmates. I'm certain they will all be better for spending a significant amount of time together. I know it works. I've seen it work, in my son's class and in other classes I've observed.

This value can be hard to explain to people who have already made up their minds. I try to tell them of the positive effect inclusion can have on the social skills and attitudes of the nondisabled students. They learn compassion, responsibility, understanding, and empathy. I have found that it is the adults who have difficulty with inclusion. Special and regular education teachers, educated and trained separately, are often resentful and afraid of change.

I have observed that Caleb's classmates are better at accepting children with differences than most adults are. His classroom peers understand why all this is so important to kids like Caleb. They help, they adapt, and—if given the proper information—they work hard to refrain from reinforcing his inappropriate behavior with laughter. They accept Caleb and his differences. After all, he is more like them than not.

I believe that these same classmates will, as adults, be more willing to live near or hire someone with a disability. I know what is possible today will be eclipsed by what is possible tomorrow when people who have enjoyed an inclusive education find it easier to make adjustments and accommodations. This belief is integral to my dedication: We do not yet know what the possibilities are.

As an advocate for inclusion, I obviously believe it is the right thing to do. At the same time, I understand why some parents don't want to take on such an awesome fight: it's too close to the heart. However difficult, I am committed to keep fighting for children's rights to a decent and respectful life.

Much of my time is devoted to advocating for families who want their child educated in a regular school setting. I am also pursuing a graduate degree in sociology. I am studying the attitudes, stigma, and prejudice associated with disabilities; these concepts greatly influence the present service delivery system and the planning and funding of future services.

If policy makers do not believe that persons with disabilities can be included, they will neither invent inclusive solutions nor see the value in funding them. If they hold the concept of segregation as *a priori,* how can they possibly understand the value of inclusive classrooms? We must stand the current paradigm on its ear and make integration of people with and without disabilities the *a priori* condition.

A note on family support: We have been fortunate to have the support that Caleb needs. He receives one-on-one help for many hours of the day and from numerous people. These helpers are integral to his growth and development and to the emotional and physical well-being of our whole family. We would not survive intact without this support. Caring for Caleb is a job that needs to be spread out among a group of committed individuals. To be sure, having such a network of support costs, but it is far less expensive than out-of-home placement.

My wife and I want Caleb with us until we all—including Caleb—agree that a change is desirable. To provide people with disabilities with a somewhat normalized life, we must take into account the needs of all family members. The most sensible way to provide support to families is to do it simply, with a minimum of regulations, and by letting families determine what is good for them.

I have been fortunate to have connected with an incredible group of professionals who work with people with disabilities in various capacities. With a vision of a progressive and humanistic future, we push to assure that appropriate community supports are in place when needed for people with disabilities. The parents and professionals in this group have become friends, and in doing so, have educated each other about their reasoning and values. And both the parents and the professionals are capable of rallying support for the other from their constituent communities.

As Caleb's father, I understand the needs of our family and other families with members who are disabled. These are needs I did not appreciate before my son's birth. Parents' opinions are necessary for positive change. Connected genetically and emotionally to our children, we can imagine possibilities that others cannot. As we are responsible for our children 24 hours a day, our view of their needs and strengths is unique, encompassing, and important. We must embrace our mission and responsibilities with the same import that doctors embrace theirs. My mission is clear: to let those who don't know see how it is, and how it can be.

Ben Adams is a freelance photographer and artist committed to inclusive education for children with and without disabilities. He has sat on various local and state special education councils and commissions in California. Currently, Ben is a member of a diverse group rewriting California state policy on Least Restrictive Environment. He is also a founding board member of a new, progressive private school that will embrace all types of diversity — gender, race, ethnicity, class, and abilities. To better understand people's attitudes and prejudices regarding disabilities, Ben is currently pursuing a Master's degree in Sociology. It is his hope to develop strategies that will positively influence society's perception of people with special needs.

The Bike

Irvin Shapell

Last summer, and for several years before, I tried to teach Jake, my ten-year-old who has Down syndrome, to ride a two-wheel bicycle. I knew he could do it physically—he is very, very coordinated. But though I tried and encouraged him, he would only take short and unsteady rides, throw his bike over, and whine to be finished. He never really wanted to try. I always had to cajole, bribe, and prod him. Jake was afraid of the bike, afraid of falling down. His solution was to avoid doing it.

Jake is not embarrassed by things that embarrass other kids, especially when he is scared. For example, he still insists on wearing "floaties" (little brightly colored plastic inner tubes worn by babies on their arms for flotation) long after all the kids he knows stopped. He is scared to swim without support (he can), even though I have worked with him to wean him from the floaties. All I accomplished with that was to make Jake afraid to get too close to me in a swimming pool. So, when I took the

training wheels off of his bike, Jake dealt with his fear
and my intrusion by simply taking to his little brother's
tricycle. He was not embarrassed to ride the trike. I was.
When I would tell him he was riding a baby trike, he
would just deny it—Jake is not wedded to my version of
reality. Although I could sometimes get him pumped to
try riding his two-wheeler, and excited to ride across our
lawn, his enthusiasm always faded.

Bike riding was just about the first thing I couldn't
teach Jake. This really bothered me.

All Jake's life, I have been the center of his world.
He lived to play with me, hang out with me, learn for
me, please me. He trusted me; I energized him. We had
fun together. I could teach Jake better than anyone else,
and could motivate him better than anyone else, even
when something scared him. I once taught him to jump
off the top of our stairs into my arms, even though he
was scared. His trust in me won out over his fear. When
Jake was young, he looked to me for everything. I felt effective—important. But the bike changed that.

As Jake continued to stick to the trike, I started to
give up on him. I began to think he would just not ever
learn to ride a bike, that he would let his fear win. Most
important to me was the fact of my own failure staring
me in the face. It was not Jake who failed to learn to
ride, but I who failed to find the right way to teach him.
I always thought I could help Jake best, but here I could
not. I felt reduced to the caricature of the overreaching
father—the obnoxious little-league dad who takes his
child's magic love of baseball and only teaches his child
that he is a failure. I felt I was pushy, nagging, and resentful of Jake's disability.

I have had a hard time letting go of Jake's normal
ghost. I got over the initial shock of his birth, and, I
thought, accepted that his differences were permanent.
But Jake approaches "normal" often; for brief moments,
I can see the kid underneath the disability, a different
kid of unlimited potential. It is so easy to imagine Jake
without the facial differences he gets from Down syndrome, wit and humor not hidden by the problems with
communication Jake has, and intelligence. Maybe if Jake
wasn't so coordinated and athletic, I would have gotten
past it by now. But Jake's refusal to ride his bike was a
constant affront to my ghost Jake.

Last year, a photographer friend of mine caught
Jake in the process of shooting a basketball. In his
photo, Jake, who is a remarkably accurate shot, is frozen
just as he is releasing the ball. Jake's arm is extended, his
hair is flying, and even his wrist is bent in follow
through. His eye is on the ball, his mouth is firm, and
there is a look of intense concentration on his face. Most
remarkable of all to me, however, the photo captures
Jake airborne—Jake is suspended in the air, and from
the way his hair is flying, he is just starting to come
down.

Without lessons, naturally, Jake shoots jump balls
and sinks them. He does not know or care how close to
perfection he comes. He does not realize or care that I
see his ghost child, the part of Jake that is pure and perfect in his running, jumping, throwing, and catching.
And he does not care that I also know that this glimpse
of the normal in Jake is just a glimpse.

Just yesterday I played street hockey with Jake. I
shot pucks at him with a hockey stick while he pre-
tended to be the goalie. After a few shots I noticed some-

thing. Like real goalies, Jake was bending his knees together to prevent the puck from sliding between his legs. It was a very subtle movement, and not something that I or anyone else had ever taught him, but it was just like what professional goalies do. It did not take special education, therapists, or endless repetition for him to "learn" this skill. He just did it, maybe by just watching a few hockey games we've been to. Yesterday I played street hockey with the ghost Jake.

I usually do not brood on Jake's disability. But I do not forget it. I do not pretend it does not exist. When Jake does something naturally, casually athletic, it lets me see—rather than just imagine—what Jake might have been like without Down syndrome. Just as I wonder how others of my kids would have been different with different personalities or looks, I wonder what Jake would have been like without Down syndrome. Watching him play soccer, shoot a basketball, or play street hockey, I think, gives me the best glimpse. Jake at his most natural and exuberant seems to strip away his disability and lets me truly see Jake without Down syndrome. There are many—too many—things Jake does that remind me of his Down syndrome and his mental retardation. Reading, math, and speech are all hard for Jake, and frustrating for me to watch him struggle to learn so slowly. Seeing him in action, seeing him learn effortlessly, balances things out for me.

That is why riding a bike was so critical. I knew Jake could do it. And I knew how he would look doing it. Smooth, fast, lit up with excitement, normal. I saw him riding with his siblings and with friends around the neighborhood. I saw him with that casual skill of his in all things physical. I had the picture in my mind already.

Riding the bike would feed his ghost child. His refusal to
even try hurt every time. I started to see creeping disability.

Last summer, we went to Maine for vacation. I took
Jake's bike, and did not take the trike, but I really did
not think he would ride it. His attempts had recently
been less frequent, shorter, and less patient. I just kept
seeing the same pattern; I just kept thinking that I could
not get Jake to do this. Sometimes I screamed inwardly
to myself, "Fine, Jake, look like an idiot if you want to,
when you are fifteen and riding a f_ _ _ _ g trike. Go
ahead, look like the worst retard stereotype." All along I
knew that Jake did not care about appearances in quite
the same way I did. Jake doesn't care about stereotypes.

One day, Jake's older sister, Anna, started encouraging Jake to ride his bike down the gentle hill of our driveway in Maine. She did it her way, prodding Jake in her
way. She used typical kid tricks that sometimes work on
Jake: "Do you love me? If you do, then ride the bike
down the driveway. If you don't I will cry" or "Jake, I
bet you can't ride that bike." Jake ain't stupid: he sees
this as the obvious ploy it is, but still loved the attention
of his older sister, and wanted to be like her. So he
started riding his bike down the driveway into Anna's
arms, and walking back up to try again, all under the
loud praise (high-fives, hugs) of his big sister. They did
this on their own—I did not even know they were trying. One day, Anna and Jake showed me what they had
done. As Jake rode down the driveway, I was proud of
them both. When I tried to tell Anna about the deep
meaning of teaching Jake to ride and about how long I
had toiled to do that, she just gave me one of those 11–

year-old smiles and shrugged. It was easy—for her. Jake
was elated. He has been riding ever since.

Anna was able to teach Jake in ways I could not.
Jake did things that I had given up on him doing. Anna
had the magic to open Jake up to a new experience. Jake
felt safer trusting her than me.

Right then and there I passed from the center of
Jake's life, and it hurt. Power (even the power to do
good things) boosts ego, and feeling it slacken worried
me. I guess we all grow up. Maybe it would be worse for
me to remain Jake's permanent center. Playing bit roles
in his growth is better than no growth. Growth is what
all the other kids do; it was why I wanted Jake to learn
to ride his bike so much.

Only Jake could conquer his fear, and I was not the
one who could help him. That's just the way it was.
Later that day, Jake went for a ride on the street. Once
his fear was gone, he hopped on his bike and rode in the
casual, naturally coordinated way he does everything.
Without the fear, he looked like he had been riding for
years. He looked so . . . cool.

Next summer, Anna's challenge: the pool!

-----

*Irvin Shapell is the Publisher of Woodbine House, a small
book publishing company specializing in books for parents and teachers of children with disabilities. He lives in
Bethesda, Maryland, with his wife and four children:
Anna, age 12, Jacob, age 11, Jesse, age 8, and Joseph, age
4. His work in publishing books for families of children
with special needs began when Jacob was born with
Down syndrome.*

Walter at 10

Richard C. Anderson

My son Walter is ten years old, five feet two inches
tall, and has never spoken a word. Walter has autism
and Pervasive Developmental Disorder. It is hard for me
to believe that Walter has reached this double-digit milestone in what seems like a few weeks. Emotionally, I calculate Walter's age from the date of his diagnosis,
January 16, 1987, not his actual date of birth, January
11, 1984. However, this "real" birthday—Walter's
tenth—has caused me to reflect on our mutual growth
and development. It has been ten intense years. As Walter has grown and changed during the past ten years, so
have I.

My wife, Rosalynn, and I held Walter's tenth birthday party at our church for about 25 children. For a
child who has autism, Walter loves the company of
other children. He does not interact directly with them,
but he enjoys having them around him. During the
party, Walter ran around the room punching balloons

and enjoying the general chaos. Most of the time, he
dribbled his beloved basketball. He likes the feel and
sound of dribbling; he'd much rather dribble than shoot.
At home we have to limit his dribbling or he will keep it
up for hours. However, this was his party, so we let him
dribble to his heart's content.

At the party, Walter had his other favorite toy, his
Slinky. (Walter prefers the new small colorful plastic
ones over the old metal ones.) He takes his Slinky everywhere and tries to keep it in his hand at all times. At the
party, Walter had his basketball, his Slinky and his
friends running around, making as much noise as possible. All in all, a great party.

One of Walter's favorite parts of the party was after-
wards, when he got a chance to clean up and put things
in order. Walter loves order. He likes things lined up
and grouped. Objects of similar size and shape, Walter
believes, should be together, lined up side by side. So, after the party, Walter got to help with cleaning off the tables and putting the folding chairs in rows against the
wall. He loved it.

I feel a little guilty admitting that Walter's love of
cleaning up is a great help to my wife and me. After
meals, when he finishes eating, he will show us his plate
and point to the sink. If we say O.K., Walter eagerly
places all the dishes in the sink. He also likes to wash the
dishes and the feel of soapy water. During his dishtime
ritual, for reasons known only to Walter, he may decide
that computer disks, mail, and full containers of sugar
must also be discarded. This aspect of an otherwise helpful compulsion is discouraging and we have to keep an
eye on him. Like most folks, we take the bad with the
good.

Walter does not talk. His receptive language, how-ever, is good and he has a limited sign language vocabu-lary. Walter's report card (officially known as the Report of Student Achievement and Effort) reports his mental age at two and a half years old and his Instructional Grade Level as "Pre-K." When I see these words, I si-lently shout, "Pre-K! Pre Kindergarten at ten!" It is hard to see these words in print. Walter's report card brings me face to face with his disabilities in a cold way. I feel that this report is a statement about how the outside world evaluates my son. Most of the time we treat Wal-ter like a normal child, but his report card—and the mea-ger expectations it conveys—is a harsh reminder of what we are facing in our attempts to prepare him for the fu-ture.

Reading Walter's report card is a surreal experi-ence. The format is similar to the reports I received in grade school; it is not designed with Special Education children in mind. Categories are adjusted to reflect the areas he is working on with his teacher. (I should say that Walter is blessed with a wonderful teacher.) Here is what he received on his last report card.

OFFICIAL	ADJUSTED	GRADE
READING	**Letters and numbers**	B
LANGUAGE ARTS Speaking	**Signs, Communication Book**	B
Written Composition	**Tracing; Matching Words**	C
Spelling	**(Not Applicable)**	\
Handwriting	**Independent Letter Writing**	D
MATHEMATICS	**Functional Concepts**	C+
SCIENCE	**Home Economics**	B
SOCIAL STUDIES	**Behavior Therapy**	B

These reports highlight the dichotomy between our home and the outside world. I love my son and see him through that love. To me, at home, he is a normal kid. We know how to communicate. I know Walter's signs, his facial expressions, and his habits. All in all, we have a great life together. However, the world, neither knowing nor loving my son, establishes these criteria and achievement categories to assess his achievement and effort. Despite their ungenerous assessment of my son, I know his achievements are great and his effort is enormous.

Walter's tenth birthday forces me to face many unanswered questions: How will we face the future? I wonder if Walter thinks about the past? Does Walter know he has autism? What would he have been like had he not been born with autism? Just who is this person who has lived with us for ten years and is now almost as tall as his mother and has never spoken to us? Who is Walter?

I have talked to many parents of children with autism. We usually discuss the value of trying to unravel the mystery of autism. We wonder whether it is important to know why our children have autism or whether it is better to just deal with autism's effects.

I've observed that those who seek answers to the "why" of autism are usually parents of children—many between eighteen months to three years—who have been recently diagnosed. I remember that stage well. When Rosalynn and I were told that Walter had autism, we went through a period of denial. We were sure that his lack of speech—at almost three years of age—was caused by a hearing problem. Once we admitted to ourselves that Walter exhibited traits of a person with autism, we moved into an intensive research phase. I assumed I could attack this problem the way I had attacked other important challenges in my life; by researching the problem and taking appropriate action. Although there were many excellent books speculating on the cause of autism, I could find nothing that definitively explained the condition or told us how to treat it. In short, I was stunned that there was no cure for Walter's autism. I found that the few researchers who do propose treatments are often embroiled in arcane debates and attacks on each others' methods. This left us feeling alone to make critical decisions about our child.

Although I still grapple with the permanency of autism, I still would like to know what causes autism, particularly if knowing the cause could help Walter. But love and time have moved me forward. Now I rarely think about cause and I never think about why. I do not feel Walter's autism is unfair to me but it is massively unfair to Walter.

I have great respect for Walter and how hard he works to learn. We work with Walter on his homework every night. He has a deep desire to learn, despite the autism that sometimes gets in the way. On occasion, his frustration with the lessons he so clearly wants to understand tears at my heart. I ache, empathizing with his frustration, yet I am incredibly proud of his efforts. I suspect Walter feels much the same way. Nothing makes him happier than hearing he completed an assignment correctly.

Walter is very sensitive about making mistakes. When I ask Walter to do something—like get a glass from the kitchen—he sometimes will come back with a fork. We then go get the glass together. I praise him and kid him about being tricked by a fork pretending to be a glass. Doing this is harder than I can describe because if he knows he has made a mistake he looks so crestfallen and frustrated. I feel he knows he knows the difference between a fork and a glass but sometimes something gets in the way. Sometimes, however, we feel that he is not trying and then we push him harder. There is a delicate balance between pushing him to progress and not discouraging him.

I often envision conversations with Walter. In these conversations Walter tells me how he feels about autism and how I can help him. These imagined conversations are long, detailed, and filled with Walter's observations about how it feels to be "inside." It helps me sometimes to think that the "real" Walter is trapped inside the "autistic" Walter. I am, however, moving toward the point of view that autism is a totally integrated part of who Walter is, not something that could be removed. Whatever caused his brain to develop the way it has is now a part of him. I hope I am wrong. I hope that in Walter's lifetime a cure will be found, or a treatment that will greatly ameliorate autism, but I am not optimistic.

This is a touchy subject. In fact some parents eschew the term "autistic child" preferring "child with autism." I think they feel that a child who has autism may someday be a child who does not have autism. To me, an autistic child is a child whose autism cannot be severed from the essence of the child's nature. I hope Walter is a child with autism rather than an autistic child. I struggle with accepting autism's effects on Walter or fighting them on every front.

Again, who is this Walter I love so much? Does autism keep me from knowing, loving, and helping my son? I so want to climb inside his mind for a day. I want to be sure that I am doing all that is possible to prepare him for the future. Sometimes I wonder: if autism could be cured or if Walter's brain could be rewired to remove the impediments to development, expression, and sociability, who would emerge? Would I know this "new" Walter?

Despite the mystery of his disorder, I think I know my son pretty well. Not just in the sense of predicting what he will do in most circumstances. And not just how he will respond to different stimuli. I think I have a pretty good handle on his personality. While I was worrying about his communication and adaptation to society, Walter was developing a unique, intriguing personality. He is, for instance, impish with a subtle sense of humor; he is ironic and playful. He is also narcissistic and vain. He knows he is handsome and he likes to dress up and look at himself in the mirror. If the autism went away, I assume these and other traits would not change. However, I am sure new, profound traits would also surface. What would they be? If he could talk tomorrow, what would he say? How would he evaluate our efforts to teach and help him for the last ten years? I feel I am close to a resolution of these questions. Or perhaps a better word is rapprochement. I do not dwell on them but they do pop into my mind from time to time.

Besides autism, Walter has Pervasive Developmental Delay. Thus, besides having the quirks caused by his autism, Walter is intellectually much younger than his physical age. I don't like the word retarded and I do not apply it to Walter. While his intellectual development is slow in some ways, in other ways, he is right on target. Like the pride in his appearance I mentioned before. At

ten his wanting to look nice is right on time. His love of
stylish clothes and his knowledge of what is "in" fasci-
nates me.

Lately, Walter has begun vocalizing in response to
our talking to him. Although they are still just sounds,
they are more appropriate than the meaningless vocal
tics he had when he was younger. He appears intent on
increasing the palate of communication tools at his dis-
posal. His voice seems to be a new discovery for him. It's
as if he is experiencing it for the first time.

I often tell Walter someday he will talk to Daddy.
We have our own private sign for this. He touches his
forehead with his forefingers and I touch my chest. I say
I know the words in his mind will come to my heart. I
say "Daddy knows." I do not know if he understands
but he likes it when we do this, usually when he first gets
in bed. That is when we "talk."

When he is tucked in bed I tell him his favorite
story, based on a real incident. In our story Walter wants
to go to McDonald's but Daddy is so tired. Finally,
Daddy says OK and we go to get McNuggets. We get
enough McNuggets for Mamma to have some, but when
we get home Walter has eaten all the nuggets and there
are none for Mamma! For some reason he loves this
story. I tell it with grand gestures and he smiles and gig-
gles. It feels so good to do these things that "get
through" to him, even if I don't know why or how.

On Saturdays I take Walter to my office and he
helps me work. He brings me documents from the
printer and carries files to my secretary's desk. Of
course, he also gets to organize my desk. My desk is usually a mess and he makes a dramatic difference by
straightening out the books, papers, my in-box and so

forth. Walter really enjoys these office visits and so do I. He really helps me and I lavish praise on him. He even uses the "very good" sign (slapping the back of the right hand into the palm of the left) when he completes a task. The first time he did this, I realized (with a lump in my throat) that he was expressing pride in his work. A small, but significant step forward in communications.

At home, at school, and in the community, I know Walter fights and works hard to do things other kids his age take for granted. It reminds me that I must fight and work just as hard. When I was young I was not a good student and I remember how stressful and humiliating it was to make mistakes in class. I remember the constant fear of being called on. I was afraid of messing up in front of my classmates, all of whom I thought were smarter than I. I wonder if Walter feels that way all the time. I know he is apprehensive when given a task he has just learned, or is not sure about.

Sometimes, I will give Walter a task I know he can complete, just so he can successfully complete it and feel good. For example when he points to something he wants (such as candy), I will ask him: "How you say?"— our cue for him to use sign language. He will then touch his tongue (the sign for candy) and smile. I then lavish "very goods" in sign language along with the candy. He loves it.

I do not wish Walter were different—I wish society were different. I wish it did not matter that some children have disabilities. I wish a person did not need so much mental power and acuity to live a happy, fulfilling life. I wish society understood special children. I wish the world were not such a dangerous place.

Before Walter, I thought to have a disabled child must mean the end of the world for a parent; a tragedy beyond belief. When I was a boy, I would frequently see a school bus with the name Willett on the side. My friends said this bus was for the "retarded" kids. I remember looking hard at those children as the bus went past. There was nothing unusual about the children on those buses that I could see. But I felt that their disabilities must be all there was to them. I could not imagine any aspects of their personalities other than their limitations. I wondered how the parents of these children coped. I kept that feeling until Walter taught me differently. The ten years of Walter's life have been ten years of the greatest love and joy imaginable. The love I feel for Walter is so particular to him that it is impossible to imagine that same feeling for a "normal" Walter. I cannot imagine being as moved by the achievements of a typically developing child as I am with every small step Walter takes in his development. The road is not level for Walter. Every small step Walter takes is uphill.

There are many things about Walter and the autism he has that I still do not know. But I do know this: it is wonderful to have Walter for my son and to know his love. I am blessed to know such a wonderful person as Walter Richard Oliphant Anderson, my son, at 10.

Richard C. Anderson is an Attorney in Chicago, where he lives with his wife, Rosalynn, and Walter. Walter has an adult stepsister, Lillia Key. Richard holds a bachelor's degree from the University of Chicago and a Juris Doctor Degree from Northwestern University School of Law. He works for the Chicago Housing Authority, in charge of personal injury defense litigation. Richard's other inter-

ests include music (especially keyboards and woodwinds) and travel. Walter, who also loves to travel, has accompanied his parents hiking in the Isle Royale National Parks and driving the Cabot Trail in Nova Scotia.

The Loneliness of the Long-Distance Daddy

David Seerman

Got a call late the other night from the evening nurse at Cassie's residential school in Monticello, New York. I knew it wouldn't be good news: happy tidings never happen after prime time. The nurse said, "Your daughter has a stomach virus and can't hold anything down."

"Is there fever?" I said. The nurse replied, "Yes, 103.5!"

Then I said something that makes sense only in retrospect. I asked, "How's the weather?" clearly knowing storm number fourteen, a wicked *northeaster,* had just crossed upstate New York leaving more than two feet of new snow in its wake.

The nurse was cheerless: "The weather's horrible," she said. "Classes are canceled. We bring staff to the kids whenever we can."

"Thanks," I said, "speak to you soon." When I hung up the phone, I turned to my wife of 21 years and cried like a baby.

What can I say? One of my children is profoundly retarded. One of my children is so disabled she'll never walk, talk, or care for herself in even the remotest sense. She doesn't even know who we are, her parents or her siblings. A fever, a snowstorm, it doesn't really matter. Cassie is helpless and now, 150 miles away and out of deliberate choice, I've made myself helpless to help her.

My daughter, Cassandra Rae—Cassie—was born on September 24, 1984. She was our sixth child. Our first daughter died two days after her birth due to a number of defects, including anencephaly, a condition in which the brain doesn't develop. Cassie wasn't like that. She weighed 6 pounds, 8 ounces, at birth and measured 18 inches in height. When I first saw her, before the doctors made their grim prognoses, she looked perfect to me. She sported a full crop of her mother's dark hair, her eyes sparkled brown and bright, and her cheeks puffed pink and creamy. Cassie's fingers deserved particular attention. They were unusually long and tapered delicately. Our doctor gave them a squeeze and announced that Susan had given birth to a concert pianist. It was a touching moment, the last we would share for quite some time.

While there were few immediate signs of problems, our joy was eclipsed by the local medical choir at the hospital. Their recital of concerns was like a chorus of horrors made more unbearable because their findings were so subtle. They slipped into our room on a constant schedule like white-gowned phantoms, wanting blood, wanting water, taking measurements, conducting tests, stabbing, prodding, and poking Cassie day and night. We couldn't wait to escape with our precious cargo and resume our lives.

Unfortunately, deep in our hearts, we knew there was something not quite right with Cassie. Even during the course of her first day, she refused to nurse. "What's the problem?" I asked Susan. She shrugged her shoulders. "Don't worry," she consoled me, "Cassie will come around."

Cassie was nine and a half years old recently and continues to grow and develop in her own disjointed fashion. Susan and I love her and love our other five children for their patience and enthusiasm. But Cassie will never come around. Only her family can come around, rally back from despair. And we do try.

I had imagined that the presence of a child with special needs would change the character of a family. I had imagined the custodial care of a loved one would wear away the fabric that held this family together. I imagined a lot of things but since I couldn't imagine the truth except by living it, let me illustrate.

Imagine the most painful hurt in the world. Imagine it being a wound, fresh and unmendable, a wound that yields the same promise of incessant pain day after day without relief. This wound was Cassie when she was born. That feeling of hurt and anguish was ours whenever we thought about or cared for her.

I went through the traditional cycle of grief that accompanies the death of a loved one . . . . but Cassie didn't die, nor were the prospects of her passing part of

Fate's master plan. Cassie was alive: growing (though rather slowly), eating, drinking, rolling on the floor in twisted circles, reaching for objects to play with. One day, years ago, a doctor I cornered in some hospital waiting room told me the truth. "Cassie will live an abnormal life of normal duration."

These are the facts! But there are other facts we've come to know, and to accept. Here was a human being, demonstrating a full range of physical and emotional responses in a very restricted fashion, and here I was, her father, behaving like she wasn't human, wasn't made of flesh and blood. Once I understood that Cassie wasn't meant to function at *normal* levels, I tried to drop my demands and change, but not lower, my expectations for her. I began to learn to live with her and love her, and, in the process, heal. Even up till today, I'm not sure how far I've come.

Cassie's I.Q. is around 20. It explains a lot. The fact that she has cerebral palsy also contributes to our dilemma and shows why she occasionally has to be molded into a chair or a position like a clay figurine. Nevertheless, Cassie has made some significant strides over the course of time. It hasn't been all one nightmarish plateau. She currently demonstrates limited, but definite, use of her hands and arms. Both her gross and fine motor skills were called into serious question early on, but every year, Cassie keeps getting slightly better than the year before.

Despite this, every single day seemed a struggle. Cassie was often sick when she was younger, and we were rarely able to distract her from her pain. We weren't even positive if it was physical pain that she was going through, which made it all the more unbearable to me.

In the middle of the night, for no explainable reason, Cassie would start screaming. I'd go down to her room and try to comfort her. It was impossible. There was no eye contact, no response that was akin to what our other children displayed. I felt I was on thin ice in new, uncharted territory. What was I to do when Cassie screamed and screamed? Even the neurosurgeons we visited were unable to reassure us. At first it made me angry and then it made me inconsolable. My inability to engage my daughter, have her respond to my care and love, was one of the reasons that I began to consider a residential school an appropriate alternative.

At this school, they tell us Cassie can actually signal for a particular item she wishes to have: juice, a banana, cookies. However, when we bring her home, which we do often, we see little evidence of such decisiveness. Perhaps, it's her surroundings; perhaps, she needs to get reacquainted with her old world, her old environment.

Sometimes, during quiet moments, I suggest to Susan that people believe only what they want to believe. If they want Cassie to be selective with her food, then maybe her new caregivers have convinced themselves she is selective, whether she really is or not. Susan knows it's a cynical thought, and tells me that I can be just as fanciful as the next person. "Don't be so hard on people," she says. And she's right. My unmitigated honesty, with myself and with others, has brought me little satisfaction and comfort.

Cassie's birth put us on a roller coaster ride that still has many more turns and looping twists in its course before it stops and we're let off. There are times I'm so happy I want to cry the cry of relief. Other times I feel

so disenchanted, I can do nothing but laugh at the odd-
ity of my situation in an attempt to rise above it.

For practically nine years, I washed Cassie, diapered
her, fed her, dressed her, carried her around the house,
cleaned up after her, and kissed her good-bye before
sending her on the bus to her special school. I repeated
the process when she returned, ending each day with a
goodnight kiss and a careful tuck-in.

For practically nine years, I integrated Cassie into
my life. After all these years of discouragement, after all
these attempts to accept this lifetime challenge, who, but
myself, can measure what was has been gained or lost?
What I've come to suspect is this: a generous peace of
mind is the ultimate reward for those who persevere.

But I didn't persevere. I tried. On good nights, early
in the struggle, I swore to the Gods I would never let
Cassie go. On bad nights, I cursed at the Gods for not
letting Cassie go, never realizing until now that I was—
and always had been—the final arbiter, that the power
of closure always had resided within me.

But the questions burn on: Why did we give up Cassie? How could we learn to deal with Cassie's many complex, chronic problems and still accept it? Or fix it?

One very specific reason we placed Cassie in a residential setting was because Susan and I could only work
with her on a limited basis. Cassie was getting bigger and
heavier, and her needs were more demanding. The
caregivers at her school could provide much more time
and energy, and with this, we hoped to see improvement
in her responses, specifically in her eating habits.

In addition, the daily grind began to wear us down
over the years. Even Cassie's siblings began to lose interest in her as she got older. They played with her less,

and when they did, it was without the spark of joy with which they used to attend her. Adding to that was the embarrassment factor. While never overt, it was quite plain that whenever we went out as a family, my other children were uncomfortable. This was especially noticeable at school events such as plays, meets, games. It was as if we recognized our family was somehow different, and we were, by virtue of the fact that people took notice of Cassie. She made noises in public; she made a mess in public, she didn't look quite right in the public eye.

It was also difficult, and sometimes treacherous, to travel with Cassie. Our vacations were limited and exhausting. Airplanes, trains, and busses presented insurmountable obstacles. Car travel was a possibility and we traveled, almost as a means of escape, at every opportunity. But Cassie came with us, which prevented us from enjoying many of the more adventurous pleasures that travel affords. Hiking mountains, going to the beach, sailing, exploring historical sites, visiting people, going to restaurants or a movie were all filled with hazards and inconveniences.

There was also more to it than that. Simple family matters that necessitated leaving the house became a job in itself. The wheelchair was heavy and cumbersome. Squeezing it into the car and then removing it at every pit-stop—supermarket, department store, neighbor, etc.—began to take its toll on our psyche. We tried to be placid but there wasn't anything placid about what we were doing. It was all hard, manual labor, in the snow, in the rain, in the cold and the heat, and seemed to go on without end.

If Suffolk County, New York, had a network of respite facilities it might have made things easier. There
were only two viable places: one had four beds and the
other had six. Dates were booked one year in advance in
the first. The latter was pure potluck. Many, if not most,
families with a disabled child don't operate on such a
pre-planned schedule. Some families live day-by-day at
best. Along with this came the phone calls and letters.
Making contact with a state or local agency was next to
impossible. The red tape seemed to stretch on forever,
and the tangle of forms made a knot around our hearts.
Sometimes it felt like the intermediaries were doing their
best to foil all our efforts to find temporary care for Cassie.

Still, since her birth, there have been many wonderful things that have happened to my family, my wife,
and myself. The most important is that our other children are perfectly healthy and, except for that acute embarrassment, remain relatively undaunted by their sister's
affliction. The model of excellence they've presented to
us in the face of catastrophe has given Susan and me the
strength to carry on.

I must remind myself every day to recognize how
fortunate I am to have healthy children, children magnificent to look at and magnificent to be with. I admire my
children above all other people. In their innocence and
acceptance of nature's intention, no matter how unusual,
I've discovered the meaning of human dignity and the
courage to acknowledge that the only failing here has
been the failing of my own natural perception of beauty.
To my children, especially to my six-year-old Samantha,
Cassie is beautiful. To my children, Cassie is their sister,
no more, no less. I'm still learning that lesson today. And

I'm sure that tomorrow there'll be more lessons to learn. As Susan suggests, I try not to be so hard on myself.

Of course, all of what I say, I suppose, only makes me a hypocrite, even if I say Cassie's school is the best school of its kind in the entire country, which I believe it is. Despite that, I feel I'm a hypocrite and a guilt-laden one at that. I'd love to write about the rewards of sacrifice and the grandeur of new beginnings. I'd love to report that Cassie called the other day and told us that she's met a new friend named Alicia, went to McDonald's for a burger, and petted a white kitten. But I can't. I'd also love to reminisce fondly and close by saying everything has turned out all right. I have done this in other writings, all before Cassie was placed upstate last July. And I meant it as well.

But this is something new and different and I don't suppose I've adjusted yet. There is a terrible ambiguity that exists in this situation which would have been remedied a long time ago if only Cassie knew who her family was. Simply put, "What is best for *us* is best for Cassie," and not the other way around because I've assumed it doesn't matter to her. A safe place, a warm place, good food, a sturdy bed, some sights and sounds to serve as stimuli; that's all that Cassie requires to make her happy. Of course, *love* is the missing ingredient here and it is that deep, rich parental love that I feel Cassie and any other placed child can never get in any residential setting.

I also think this love is the driving force that keeps me up at night, twisting and turning, and thinking about Cassie. More and more I'm starting to believe that even though Cassie can't articulate it, she needs her parents' love and the separation is not healthy for her because that love is not always present. Therefore, "What is best for Cassie is best for us," is also an honest statement and an honest feeling.

Everything hangs in the balance now. I thought that placing Cassie would be simple. I thought I could go easier on myself and, like some splendid Sisyphus, throw off the stony burden of the last nine years. I even thought I would finally be able to spend more quality time with my other children, working on relationships long overdue, commitments long underdone. But I see clearly now that I miss her terribly. I also am beginning to see that my children benefited from Cassie's presence, that removing Cassie didn't change behaviors or even allow for more one-on-one time because it was there all along.

Susan is fond of saying, "Love is all a child really needs," and I'm beginning to finally understand what she means. Children are a composite of life experiences. My children are what they are because of Cassie and not in spite of her. Cassie has impacted all our lives in good, fine ways, in loving ways that were evident on a daily basis. I didn't need to separate Cassie from the rest of the family to make them better. My family didn't need to be purged in order to be fixed. It was never broken!

As I said before, only Susan and I wrestle with the nature of Cassie's disability and with our decision to put Cassie in school. One day we feel O.K. about it, then we'll get a call saying Cassie's has a stomach ailment and the only option is antibiotics or a Tylenol. We very rarely administered medicine to Cassie, primarily because she rarely was sick while living at home. Unfortunately, it seems to me that Cassie is frequently sick nowadays.

Finally, as do all good things, it comes back to *love* and always will. We miss Cassie and I suspect one day in the future, we just might bring her home or closer to us, permanently. Whether we build a special apartment for her above our garage or hire someone to help with the constant care she needs is of no consequence as of this moment. Our decision to place her was both *right* and *wrong* and demonstrates how perplexing and delicate choices like these are to make and accept.

Nowhere in the world was a decree ever issued proclaiming that the sixth child born to David and Susan Seerman would be born differently from other children. I've come to believe that there's no design for tragedy nor a design whereby the sins of the past return to punish the sinner. The grand design is in the intention of nature and not in the execution of its parts.

This alone makes me feel better. Why? Because this means that there's no method in the madness and sadness found here on Earth. Life is as random and unpredictable as the shape of the next snowflake, and we all must take our chances if we are to stick.

David Seerman has been married for over twenty years and currently works as a full-time father, ministering to his six children, who range in age from six to seventeen. He also works full-time as an English teacher at Shoreham-Wading River High School in Long Island, New York. In his spare time, David works as an educational consultant for the National Urban Alliance, demonstrating cutting-edge educational techniques to teachers and students alike. His articles and columns have appeared in both local and national newspapers and magazines. Born in Crown Heights, Brooklyn, David has lived with his family in Washington, D.C., Buffalo, New York, Ellsworth, Maine, Fishers Island, New York, and Bayport, Long Island.

The Sky's the Limit

Joe Greenholtz

Our oldest daughter, Emi, has Down syndrome. I wish I could say that I have "come a long way" or that I have a handle on, or the answers to, bringing up a child with a disability. After all, I've been at it for eleven years now and that is a long enough learning curve for most ventures. But, in truth, every year is an adventure. It's not that the lessons of the past don't apply, but every stage of Emi's life brings my family and me unforeseen challenges, complications, and opportunities.

We didn't find out until a few months after Emi was born that she has Down syndrome. The doctors knew, but rather than being the bearers of such "horrendous" tidings, they apparently were hoping we'd figure it out for ourselves. They must have been afraid we would shoot the messenger. There was a high despair factor implicit in that introduction to our new way of life, but we got lucky. Within days of getting the news, accompanied by the all too familiar bleak "expert" disclaimer on how

limited Emi's potential would be, Dr. Val Dmitriev of
the University of Washington came to Japan (where we
were living at the time, and are again) with a different
message, a message of hope. She introduced us to *Time
to Begin,* her book on early intervention for children
with Down syndrome and before we had had a chance
to begin a long, satisfying wallow in the self-pity and mutual recriminations that so often seem to follow the birth
of a child with a disability, we were challenged to help
Emi to explore the limits of her potential—and to believe that are no limits.

That message of hope has become a double-edged
sword. On the one hand, there is the comfort of knowing that progress, while it may be slower than for our
other kids, will always come; and it has. On the other
hand, there is the frustration that comes from feeling
that the grail of "normalcy" is always just beyond one's
grasp.

There seem to be two ways of approaching the question of aspiring to normalcy. In some circles it is considered demeaning to the child to wish that she could be
normal. That is seen as devaluing her "specialness" and
the contribution she makes to life just for being who she
is. I'm not denying that Emi is special, or that we have
learned a lot about the intrinsic value of every human
life. I have expended a lot of effort in trying to get others—primarily educators and other "professionals," not
to mention my own family—to go beyond the Down syndrome label stereotype to see Emi as the multi-dimensional person that she is. I know that the process has
made me more tolerant of differences in others. However, it would be dishonest to say I wouldn't give up
those benefits if I could wave a magic wand and erase

that extra chromosome. Since that is not in the cards, I have chosen to believe that we shouldn't accept Emi as she is, or rather as she appears to be for the moment.

The hallmark of a human being is adaptability, which is another way of saying the ability to learn. I think it is nothing more than a comforting delusion to accept limitations and lowered expectations as being best for your child. It absolves you from fighting for more. If we weren't driven by the idea of normalcy, by the idea that Emi can achieve what others take for granted—a job, independent living, a social life—we probably would have succumbed to "expert" advice a long time ago.

My wife and I, although we agree that Emi should constantly be challenged to achieve more, seem to approach it from different angles. Hiroko worked constantly with Emi until our second child was born. She read to her, talked to her, helped her to learn how to sit and crawl, to eat with a spoon, and to express her needs. As a result, she seems to be more in tune with Emi's rhythms and learning patterns and less likely to get frustrated with Emi than I am. She deserves the credit for laying the foundation for Emi's continuing progress. I, on the other hand, sometimes start foaming at the mouth when Emi can't seem to get something that (I feel) should be easy for her. If she can run the VCR and handle my computer, why does she still add on her fingers?

I probably react the way I do because Emi functions within normal ranges in so many ways. She is *so* close. The downside of refusing to be satisfied with the status quo is that one tends to focus on what is lacking instead of what has been achieved. Emi's accomplishments are considerable and we have never been given reason to be-lieve that she has reached the outer limits of her poten-tial. She is English ·Japanese bilingual (her mother and many of our friends are Japanese) and reads both, Eng-lish at grade level. We started her on the Suzuki violin method when she was 3 years old and although her younger siblings have both since surpassed her she con-tinues to progress, at her own pace, but steadily. She loves to play in front of an audience and has been in quite a few recitals. She has recently started piano and ballet. On land she has a certain awkwardness that comes with hypotonicity and lacks stamina. But put her in the water and she swims as well as most kids her age.

Her social skills are excellent and she reads people's feelings very well. By way of illustration, I remember be-ing out trick or treating with her on Halloween. Emi would go into someone's hallway and while she was waiting for her treats she would say things like, "My, what a lovely home." The homeowner, looking some-what harassed from having spent the last several hours shoveling candy into kids' bags, would invariably beam with pleasure and stop to chat. That is something that I certainly never taught her and she often catches me by surprise with some little kindness or remark that I hadn't expected from her.

Emi has always preferred the company of adults. It is when she is with her peers that she seems out of place, childish. As she approaches her teen years, this is becom-ing a bigger concern for us. We try to find ways to inte-grate her into peer-group social activities, but it's a kind of vicious circle. The weaker her social skills are, the less enthusiastic she is about mixing with other kids her own age. That kind of social interaction can be exhausting.

You always have to be on your toes, up on what's popular and hip, quick on your feet—even at age eleven. Yet there are many people who are awkward with their peers, who go through a sometimes lonely, sometimes painful adolescence to emerge into adulthood.

And in many ways this time of life is more painful for those of us watching from the sidelines. I know how cruel children can be—and remember how cruel I myself was to some of the kids from my past. And I know my heart would break if someone called Emi a "retard" or ostracized her.

As she approaches teenage years, Emi is starting to fall in love. This is something that happens to every little girl, but there are implications for Emi that don't apply to all those others. Right now we are dealing with "puppy love" and there will probably be a few heart breaks along the way. But in the age of AIDS, the anguish of puppy love could give way, in time, to real tragedy. She is extremely stubborn when it comes to doing something she has her heart set on. I'm not sure whether I can teach her to protect herself and I know that I can't always be there to protect her myself. That is scary.

We've been lucky to find teachers who weren't put off by the fact that she has Down syndrome and were willing to treat her as an individual instead of a stereotype. I shudder to think what her education would have been like had we chosen to remain in Japan as "civilians." (We are back in Japan with the Canadian Foreign Service and the Canadian government funds education equivalent to Canadian standards.) In Tokyo, there is an elementary school which has a unit for children with disabilities about ten yards from our house. It presently has 8 students ranging in age from 1st to 6th grade and 3 teachers assigned to it. The program requires all the students to do the same things together all the time. Given the teacher-student ratio, one would think they could individualize the program, but this is not the case. We have friends with children with Down syndrome in other Japanese schools. Although schools will place children with disabilities into regular classrooms if the parent insists, the reception they have received ranges from teachers who make program modifications on their own time (no teachers' aides or other help is provided) to teachers who continuously ask pointedly "When do you intend to take your child out of my class? His presence is causing a disturbance."

Even this, however, is enlightened compared to the middle (junior high) school for handicapped children in Tokyo, which is something out of the 19th century. The curriculum (which the principal proudly points out has a long and distinguished history dating back before World War II) calls for the students to spend at least 3 hours a day in a chair working on some task like needlepoint to train them to be able to stay in one place for long periods of time, a skill they will need in the workforce!

Emi goes to a segregated school in Tokyo. It has a 3:1 student-teacher ratio and offers the whole spectrum of specialized services, physical, speech and occupational therapy, beyond an individualized educational program. We wanted Emi to have an English-language education but the international schools begged off from mainstreaming her. This was despite the fact that she had been mainstreamed in her neighborhood school in Canada and we were willing to supply a teacher's aide. All of this was frustrating because conversations with school officials basically ended—except for the pleasantries—as soon as I said "I have a daughter with Down syndrome and . . ." We believe that we have gained in program quality what we have sacrificed in integration. What else could we believe and still sleep at night?

We haven't given up on integration, though. Emi's teachers have actively tried to arrange inclusion opportunities for her with our full support. Over the past year, she has taken art classes once a week at the American School. In April of this year, she started attending a regular fourth-grade class at the school her siblings attend, one day a week. If it works out there's a good chance it can continue in the new school year.

That news made Naha, Emi's younger sister, a little squirmy. The thought of having her sister, who still does math on her fingers, in the same school did not appeal to her. We talked about why she was uncomfortable with the idea and I think she agrees that plusses for Emi outweigh the possible minuses for her. Only time will tell.

This is a difficult time for Naha. In almost every way, besides age, Naha is the older sister. She is bright and capable and takes things seriously. She has known for a long time that Emi was different, but did not know how or why. Over the past little while I've taken her aside to explain about Down syndrome. I was grateful that I haven't had to give her the "there but for the grace of God go thou" lecture, but that hasn't stopped her from being embarrassed by Emi from time to time. Especially where her own peer-group acceptance is on the line. The kids in the neighborhood come to call for Naha, but almost never for Emi. I know that bothers Emi, but at the same time she seems somehow relieved to be excused from the pressures of competing with her sister and with her peers. For her part, Naha does try to include Emi and to 'protect' her when they are together.

Our family life is complicated, but I hope enriched, by the fact that I'm in the Foreign Service. Since we can't take it for granted that Emi would be accepted into the local or international school system wherever we might be posted, a lot of careful consideration goes into choosing where we can serve. Our original inclination was to give up foreign-service life for the stability of home. We discussed it among ourselves and sought the advice of those we had come to trust. Among those was Pat Oelwein, from the University of Washington's Down Syndrome Program. She told us that if we let Emi's disability dictate how we lived our lives we would become a "disabled family" instead of a family with a member who happens to have a disability. Others told us we should forget the foreign service and just keep Emi in Ottawa because we'd never find the same type and quality of education elsewhere. We'll never know, without the benefit of hindsight, whether we have made the right choices for her and for the rest of our family.

"Only time will tell" might as well be the family motto. Many are the nights I have found myself lying awake wondering whether Emi will be able to find a satisfying job, live independently, and handle her own finances. I wonder if she will ever marry and worry about who will look after her if she outlives us, as now seems likely.

On the other hand, I've got great hopes for Emi. I think that she will graduate from high school and go on to a community college, or dare I say it, some kind of university program. She is part of a generation of young people with Down syndrome who have benefited from early and consistent education and who have been challenged all their lives to keep pushing the limits. I'm confident that this group will smash the stereotypes of limited horizons and low achievement and that Emi will be at the front of the parade. But still, if I could get a hold of that magic wand . . . .

Joe Greenholtz was born in Winnipeg, Canada in 1955. After graduating from the University of Winnipeg he worked as a taxi driver, blackjack dealer, and carnival barker. He moved to Japan in 1979 and started teaching English, pausing only long enough to get married, father three children, and complete an M.Ed. at Temple University (Japan). Given his somewhat checkered past, Joe is constantly amazed to find himself in Canada's diplomatic service at the Canadian Embassy in Tokyo.

If Not Always the Victor, Always the Hero

Henry Jay Karp

I always thought foreshadowing was merely a literary device used by particularly unimaginative writers. Life is not so neatly packaged as to hand us intriguing little hints of what the future holds in store. I always thought that. That was until Joshua, our son with autism, was born.

I cannot say that my wife's pregnancy was seriously problematic, especially compared to others I have seen. Gail experienced no bleeding; no paralysis. She was not restricted to bed rest for months on end. But I can say that it was challenging. She had experienced a particularly hard fall which provided us with quite a few anxious moments. There were more than the usual aches and pains; three false labors; and finally, the need for a drug-induced delivery.

Joshua was difficult coming into this world, and once he arrived, somehow I sensed that the difficulty had just begun. From the day of his birth, Joshua seemed cool and indifferent. I remember how disappointed I was at his lack of response. When Shira, our eldest, was born, I looked down at her and she looked up at me, and we bonded instantly, right then and there in the delivery room. But not so with Josh. It would be months before we made any sort of spiritual connection.

Today, I do indeed believe in foreshadowing. For the challenges of the months preceding Joshua's birth, and of the birth itself, were but a foretaste of what was yet to come.

When Joshua was born, we lived in San Jose, California. I was serving a congregation which was, to say the least, demanding. In the world of religion, there are some congregations that expect their minister, priest, or rabbi to be nothing short of messianic. A mere mortal will never do! Unfortunately, my congregation was one of them. The pressures placed upon me were enormous. Foolishly, my response was to fall into their trap. Whatever I gave this congregation, it wasn't enough. So I would turn around and give them more. I was being wholly consumed. I had no time, no energy, and all too little place in my life for my family. Like a sponge, the congregation absorbed all that I had.

Needless to say, this wreaked havoc on my family life, especially on my relationship with my wife. We came as near to getting a divorce as I ever wish to be. So it was neither surprising nor illogical when she discounted any concerns I expressed about Joshua. When I shared with her my feelings of how he seemed unattached, she was quick to retort that it was not Joshua, but I who was unattached. And of course, the truth stung.

When I shared my concerns with our doctor, there, too, I received little support. "Don't worry," he said. "Different children develop at different rates." Yet I sensed that something was seriously wrong. It just seemed unnatural for a healthy child to be indifferent to cuddling. It just seemed inappropriate for a one-year-old to wake up at two o'clock every morning, screaming inconsolably. I was convinced that something must be awry when a little boy with loving parents and an affectionate sister would go through his day apparently oblivious to those around him. Still, I was told that the problem was mine, and not his.

Joshua had just turned two when we moved to Davenport, Iowa. Before assuming my new pulpit, we took a little vacation with my wife's family. We went to a favorite spot of ours, Traverse City, Michigan, where my wife and her siblings had spent many beloved summers at Interlochen, the National Music Camp. One day, while strolling the grounds of the camp, my father-in-law asked if Joshua had any difficulty in hearing. So often, he just failed to respond when people spoke to him. Right there on the spot we contrived and conducted our own crude hearing tests. Through them, we arrived at the conclusion that it was not that Joshua was deaf, but just that he was selective about what he chose to hear. We all laughed at this willful little boy. But Gail's and my laughter was hollow, for we had come to share our concerns over Josh. We agreed that as soon as we were settled in Davenport, we would investigate this matter.

We arrived in Davenport the second week in July of 1985. That very same week, we embarked upon the grueling and frightening odyssey that would eventually lead us to the harsh reality of Joshua's diagnosis as being a person with autism. It started with his pediatrician, who sent us to a program which tests very young children for hearing loss. Having determined that his hearing was fine, these people sent us to the local agency which administers educational programs for children with special needs. After making one home visit, their observer determined that Joshua's presenting concerns were behavioral, communication, and stress in the home. *Stress in the home!* Imagine how that made us feel! Of course there was stress in our home. We had just moved, and moving is stressful. Indeed, we had come to Iowa to escape the stress of our California life. On top of that, we had a two-year-old son whose behaviors seemed more and more bizarre with each passing day. Now we were being told that stress in our home was a contributing factor to our child's obviously dysfunctional behavior. GUILT! It has to be one of the most potent of stressors!

This home visit resulted in our being referred to a multi-disciplinary evaluation team. In the meantime, Joshua's behavior became more and more frustrating for us. He was expelled from a local preschool because he insisted upon climbing the bookshelves. Why was this child so unruly? Why didn't he respond to us? Why was he so different from his sister? What were we doing wrong with him? These and other questions plagued us mercilessly. We seesawed between feelings of anger and despair, frustration, and confusion.

It was the end of October before we met with the multi-disciplinary evaluation team. The team was composed of a social worker, a speech pathologist, a psychologist, and an educational consultant. As a result of that meeting, two very important steps were taken. First, the team agreed to arrange for a special education teacher to come to our home, to work with Josh. Second, they referred us to a psychiatrist at the local community mental health center. (Little did I know as we entered the mental health center on that chilly November night, that I would eventually serve as president of the board of that center. Foreshadowing is a fickle phenomenon!)

It was that psychiatrist who was the first to speak to us of this thing called "autism." I had never heard the word before, and neither had my wife. As he spoke, I fell into shock. My son was sick! He had somehow contracted this terrible infirmity! How do things like this happen?

To this day, I do not know whether the psychiatrist misspoke when he described autism, or I just could not comprehend it all, being so stunned by the revelation. Whichever it was, I left that meeting mistakenly believing that while autism is a lifelong disability, it can be completely compensated for through proper education and training. Josh was going to be all right! He just had to learn to work around this autism business!!!

The psychiatrist informed us that his diagnosis was only preliminary, and that nothing was certain. For certainty, Josh required a thorough evaluation at the Department of Child Psychiatry at the University of Iowa Hospitals. So the appointment was made.

We took Joshua to Iowa City for this "authoritative" evaluation on February 7, 1986. It is a date we will always remember, like a birthday or an anniversary, but of course, without the joy. Joshua took tests. We took tests. It was a full day: doctors, psychiatrists, psychologists, social workers, therapists of every variety. And then came the big consultation at the end. Yes, Josh was a person with autism. In their opinion, the degree of his autism ranged from moderate to severe. Then they dropped the bomb. We were told that 97 percent of those with autism, and especially those as severely afflicted as was Josh, ultimately needed to be placed in institutions. To say that both Gail and I were stunned would be an understatement. Indeed, calling it an understatement is itself an understatement. We were absolutely devastated! In a choking voice, I asked about what I had thought the local psychiatrist said. "Can't he be taught to compensate for it?" "Only up to a point," I was told. Joshua would always be challenged by his autism. He would always be different because of it. In all likelihood, he might never be able to function effectively in society.

The anguish of it all! My son—not destined to go to college! My son—not destined to transform the world with the gifts of his mind, the warmth of his heart, and the works of his hands! My son—the bearer of the family name, to become the last of the line of Karp; never to know the thrill of romantic love, the fulfillment of marriage, and the miracle of parenthood! When we bring children into this world, there is so much we take for granted. The blessings of a "typical" life, we do not envision as blessings, but as our children's birthright. At that horrible moment, my wife and I sat helpless as we witnessed our son being stripped of that birthright. What would become of him, his future now uncharted?

Yet even in the darkness of our despair, a new light
was beginning to dawn. All of a sudden, Joshua had
been transformed. No longer was he that incorrigible little imp. No longer was he the fount of my frustration.
No. There was something heroic about him. He had become a little warrior, waging a tireless battle against a relentless adversary. His was the struggle to live his life as
best he could. That he was battling forces beyond him—
beyond us all—forces he could never come to comprehend, mattered little to him. He would continue to
explore and expand, albeit at a slower pace than others,
and albeit down a twisted trail, but continue he would.
It was at that moment that we bonded; the bonding so
long delayed, but so well worth the waiting.

Yet in truth, Joshua did not change at all. He was
the same little boy who insisted upon scaling the shelves
of the preschool. Rather, it was I who had changed. It
was I who had opened up. The little hero was always
there, always the hero. It was I who was late in perceiv-
ing it.

Once parents of children such as Josh move beyond
the shock of the initial revelation of their child's condition, they find that they are forced to choose how they
will respond to that new reality in their lives. Some will
choose the path of denial—"Not my child! There has
been some mistake!" Others will choose the path of iner-
tia—"If I do nothing, perhaps it will go away, like a passing phase." Still others will choose the path of passive
advocacy—"Please, tell me what to do, where to go, and
who to see." The possibilities are endless.

Practically from the moment of diagnosis, Gail and I
chose the path of resistance—resistance to the status
quo. While we accepted Joshua's diagnosis, we refused

to accept the inevitability of his sentence to eventual in-
stitutionalization. If 97 percent of all the people with
autism were eventually institutionalized, then we would
do everything in our power, and beyond our power, to
place Joshua in that other 3 percent.

In this quest, Gail boldly assumed the mantle of family leadership. Being the consummate researcher, she understood that before we could act effectively on Josh's
behalf, we needed to be informed. Therefore, she took it
upon herself to ferret out every available piece of information about our adversary, autism. She read books and
articles, and she wrote letters—lots and lots of letters;
letters to any individual and any institution whose name
she came across in her research. And she got lots and
lots of answers. With each response came more information, more insights, more questions, and new directions.

"Knowledge is power," the old adage goes. Gail and
I have always lived by that rule. Indeed, it is fundamental to our own professional lives. Yet never more than at
this time did we plumb the depths of its meaning and appreciate the profundity of its wisdom. The more we
learned, and the more contact we had with knowledge-
able others, the more we felt back in control of Joshua's
destiny.

As a result of one of Gail's letters, we received an in-
vitation to have Joshua undergo a month long in-patient
evaluation at U.C.L.A.'s Neuropsychiatric Institute. We
scheduled the evaluation for July of 1986. As fate would
have it, that particular month would turn out to be a particularly traumatic time in my life. When we left for California, I did not know that my mother, who was living
in Florida, was dying of cancer. My parents had intentionally decided to keep that information from me. They

did not want me to cancel the Los Angeles trip so that I could be with her. Even they did not realize how near was her end. One evening, while we were in California, my sister called to tell me the truth. I was torn. At whose side should I be? By my mother or by my son, both in their times of need? "Stay with Josh," my sister and father counseled. "That's how Mom would want it." I knew they were right. That is how my mother would have wanted it. For her, there was nothing as sacred as the family, and no duty as absolute as the duty of a parent to his or her children. So I found myself in a race with the clock. After our business was concluded at U.C.L.A., and I had seen my family safely home to Iowa, would I still have time to scoot down to Florida and be with my mother, to say good-bye?

These were the questions that plagued me as Gail and I sat in the office of Joshua's attending psychiatrist, listening to his final evaluation.

"Your son exhibits the characteristics of someone with severe autism," he said.

"What does that mean? What should we do?" we asked.

"Nothing." he responded. "Just take him home and enjoy him while you still have him."

"You mean there is nothing we can do for him?"

"Nothing. There are certain parts of his brain that simply do not function. For example, if I handed him a ten dollar bill and set him down in the middle of West-wood Plaza (a shopping area just outside the U.C.L.A. campus) he would starve to death. He simply would never be able to understand that he could take that ten dollar bill and use it to buy food. So take him home and enjoy him while you can. Soon enough you will have to institutionalize him."

I was filled with anger and with pain. How much tragedy can one person take at one time? I was losing my mother. Now this fellow was telling me that I was going to lose my son. That evening, Gail and I resolved not to blindly accept this psychiatrist's verdict. Perhaps he was right, and there was nothing we could do for Joshua. Even so, that did not free us from our responsibility to try. As it says in *The Ethics of Fathers,* one of the sacred texts of our faith: "While it is not incumbent upon you to complete the task, neither are you free to desist from it." We would not desist. As long as we had the strength, the resources, and the opportunity, we would pursue every possible option. While we could live with the failure of our attempts, we could never live with our own failure to try.

From that day to this, we have continually explored many avenues which have offered the promise of a better life for Josh. We have experimented with drugs such as Fenfluramine and Ritalin. We have had him tested for brain allergies. We have put him on an "elimination diet." We have dabbled in facilitated communication. We had him undergo auditory training. And the list goes on. Many of these were more or less dead ends, but some of them were remarkably effective. None provided us with a miracle cure, but then again, we did not expect them to. If these experiences have taught us anything, they have taught us the value of trying. With each attempt, Joshua has grown a little; his universe has expanded.

It has been this philosophy which we have carried to his educational settings as well. Constantly, we have insisted that his teachers, his therapists, and especially those administrators who oversee his education, push the outside of the envelope. Let us not dwell on what Joshua cannot do. Let us find out what he can do. If there are doors in his brain which appear to be locked, and we cannot find the key, then let us use the battering ram. Let us force those doors open with creativity and with challenge.

Today, he is a very different little boy than he was when he was at UCLA. He is more open, more loving, more giving, more social. His favorite playmate is his older sister, and the love between them is delightfully obvious. And now, he has a younger sister as well, a baby. We worried about how he would accept this new presence in our home, but our worries were for naught. For with her, he is both remarkably affectionate and surprisingly gentle. Though nowhere near being a silvertongued orator, he does have communication skills. He loves to laugh and to sing, and has even developed an entertaining sense of humor, replete with practical jokes. And as far as that psychiatrist's parable of the ten dollars goes, if he saw Josh today, I think he would have to retract it. After all, this little boy, like all eleven-year-old boys, has discovered that quarters can be magically transformed into moments of delight in front of a video game.

Yes, Joshua has come a very long way. He has fought many a battle. And if not always the victor, he is always the hero. What will his future hold? God only knows. But this I do know. His future is very much in the making. What I do; what my wife does; what his teachers do; what Josh does—the choices we make, the actions we take—these more than anything else, even more than the autism itself, will determine what that future will be.

One final thought. I know that this was supposed to be an essay from the unique perspective of a father. Perhaps in providing that uniqueness, I have failed. I have spoken far more in the first person plural—"we"—meaning my wife and myself, than I have in the first person singular, "I." I have done so on purpose. For if there was but one message I would wish to communicate to fellow fathers of children with special needs, it is the message of "we." When it comes to meeting those special needs of our children, fathers cannot do it alone, and neither can mothers. As our children need us by their side and on their side, so do we need each other. To face the challenges which lie before us, we need the strength of our wives, and they need ours, and our children need us working on their behalf together.

Rabbi Henry Jay Karp serves Temple Emanuel of Davenport, Iowa. He is married to his cantor, Gail Posner Karp, whom he met while they were students at the Hebrew Union College-Jewish Institute of Religion, in New York City. They hold the distinction of being the first romance and marriage of fellow students from that seminary. They have three wonderful children, Shira, 13, Joshua, 11, and Helene, who is almost a year old. Rabbi Karp has served congregations in New Rochelle, New York, Lincoln, Nebraska, and Los Gatos, California, as well as the one he serves at present. He is active in both Jewish and secular affairs nationally as well as in his local community.

My Inspiration and Hope

Harrison Dixon

My son's bus pulled up in front of our house and before the wheelchair lift had hit the ground, Mark announced that he was running for student council president. He was so excited and animated. I, on the other hand, was uneasy with the whole idea. The image of my son rolling his wheelchair around school and asking for votes did not sit well with me. I grew up in a home where we were taught never to ask anyone for anything. I didn't know what to say.

Before I could offer an opinion, Mark was at his computer, telling me that he had to make banners and buttons and write a campaign speech. I wanted to turn off the computer and try to talk some sense into him. Who would vote for a boy who could not walk, could barely feed himself, and had trouble sitting up? How could he win a student council election?

My wife, who was more optimistic about his chances, helped Mark write a campaign speech. He practiced his speech until he could recite it from memory.

I dreaded the election day. The morning of the election, despite my stress, Mark was already awake, grinning from ear to ear. "Today is election day!" he shouted gleefully. His face beamed and my heart sank. I did not want him to be disappointed by losing an election when winning seemed such a long shot. I worried how he would handle defeat.

I left work early to be there for him when he got home. I thought we would go out and have a fast food treat to help him get over losing. When I heard his bus coming, I went out to wait for him. The bus door opened, and he started clapping his hands, yelling, "I won, I won." The bus driver announced, "I didn't know I would be driving the presidential limo today."

Had reality gone on vacation? How could he have won? The bus driver and his assistant were all smiles. "Aren't you proud of him?" one said. He was so full of himself that I had to hold his hand to get him to stop talking long enough to bid the bus driver good-bye.

Together, we attended a summer student council camp with officers from other schools. The majority of the activities were designed for children who could stand up, cheer, sing, and do various marches. Though they were very kind to us, Mark and I found ourselves watching the cheering and marching instead of actively participating.

My life is divided into two periods and the dividing line is clear and distinct: the birth of my son, Mark. Pronounced dead by an obstetrician and baptized twice at two hospitals, Mark decided to survive being born six-

teen weeks prematurely. Now 11 years old, Mark has a
multitude of physical challenges that require awesome
amounts of time, resources, and energy.

His birth was the first leg of an emotional roller
coaster that I continue to ride. When he survived the on-
slaught of problems associated with an extremely prema-
ture birth, we knew that Mark would be challenged in
some way. Over the years, we have constantly re-as-
sessed our expectations: most of our revisions for
Mark's physical abilities have been downward. As he
grew, I saw that there were many physical skills that
Mark would likely never master.

As Mark gets older, I find that his mother's perceptions and mine diverge. As a man looking at a manchild,
I have concerns that she can only imagine. At the age
when I would have expected to teach him how to hunt
and fish and to take him to baseball games, I find myself
teaching him how to hold a cup to his mouth.

As he approaches his teenage years, I can see his
personality developing and trying to express itself
through obstacles presented by his physical disability.
Sometimes, Mark will say or do something that my father or my grandfather or I would be expected to do,
and, for a brief moment, he is a perfect representation of
one of his forefathers. It's as if our genes are emerging in
his spirit. His physical disability causes him to uncon-
sciously mimic my father and grandfather as I remember
them as old men.

Sometimes, I try to understand what goes on in his
mind. He usually seems happy with the trappings of his
world, the things that he can manage, handle, and control. I worry that maybe he is too happy with his little
controlled world. For instance, sometimes I feel he

should be outside, following his dad around, doing the things that men do. Yet Mark seems content to be in the kitchen, reading recipes to his mother. I wonder: does he enjoy these activities because it's what he wants to do or because it is all he can do? Are our spirits pruned by our circumstances? Do we all find contentment in what we can do well and exclude all others?

I find myself wondering if the relationship and the activities that fathers and sons share are all that important. Then I find myself rebelling against that thought. I have seen men who have taken comfort in this fantasy lose a precious relationship, and, feeling unnecessary, become absentee fathers.

A child's challenges ask much of each family member, but the emotional toll may be greatest on the father. As a father, often I am placed in situations that require mindsets that are new for many, if not most men. While nurturing comes naturally to my wife, I have had to learn it with few role models to follow.

Often, I fail miserably at the nurturing that I am called upon to provide. It is a challenge for me to do things that mothers often do with children, especially disabled children. I must manipulate my schedule to take Mark to almost all of his dental appointments. Once at the dentist's, I even find it difficult to make small talk with the mothers in the waiting room. Yet, on other occasions, I find I am also phenomenally successful at tasks that I never expected to have to perform as a father, such as persuading Mark to eat when he is exerting his few options of control—refusing to eat.

Society seems to have tidy little pockets of expectations for fathers' roles. Often, when I push Mark's wheelchair in front of a group of mothers, I feel their eyes follow us as if to say "Where is his mother?" Being an African-American male only adds to the confusion. Given the stereotypical opinions many people have, it must be disconcerting, if not astonishing, to see an African-American man care for a child with severe disabilities.

Sometimes, Mark's entire family shows up for his various appointments. We all go in and sit together in the waiting room, then we all go to the examining room together. Most health care providers gladly accommodate us: those who don't never see us again.

I have learned so much from my son. He has taught me the true worth of the individual. I have learned to separate one's true spirit from the physical case into which we have been born. His unique perspective allows him to be absolutely honest about everything and he manages to see humor where most of us cannot.

Mark meets each day with joy and anticipation. Somehow, he never seems to be down or concerned about his circumstances, physical or otherwise. Watching the gusto with which Mark meets each day gives me a new form of courage to face life's little challenges.

Yet, there have been dark, rudderless days, filled with uncertainty and anger. I developed a kind of controlled rage that seems ever-present. After I realized that anger was consuming me both body and soul, I learned to direct it positively. Once directed, anger became a friend, a good friend. I learned to use channeled anger to overcome fear and anxiety in order to keep my family together and get needed services for Mark.

Sometimes, it feels as if it is only this rage that keeps me sane. I seem to have two choices: accept adverse circumstances or fight back. I fight back. I can remember having to make difficult decisions regarding professional advancements that would require travel and long hours and would interfere with my ability to be there for Mark's therapies and many needs. My judgments are not based on what is best for me, or even for my family, but what is best for Mark. Sometimes I think about what might have been, and I must admit it angers me.

I have found that service providers do not understand committed fathers. Perhaps because they believe fathers are not as gentle as mothers, they are more likely to acquiesce to their requests. I find they do not expect fathers to be either rational or reasonable; they appear to forgive fathers for all sins except being lukewarm about commitment to their family.

On the whole, my workplace has been gracious about allowing me leave to attend my son's many appointments. Once they refused, and I went anyway. Later, my supervisor told me to do whatever I had to when Mark was sick. I think the world forgives fathers for being fathers.

Sometimes I think about how my son's disability affects my other child. At the age of 15, Reuetta has been wonderful about the whole thing. She helps him, tolerates his teasing, and is very patient with her "little brother" as she affectionately calls him. She has been deprived of a typical sibling relationship and all that goes with it. I also worry about Mark depending on her when we are no longer around. I often wonder how it would have been to watch my children grow up under "normal" circumstances, whatever those are. I know that to some extent, parenting is a game of chance, yet I frequently see families in crisis for reasons other than the circumstances of birth.

There are many moments that I actually feel that Mark is a gift because of the outpouring of humanity that springs forth whenever he meets people. From the beginning, my wife and I have tried hard to instill in Mark a sense of dignity, seasoned by a great deal of discipline. We knew that whatever he would become in life, despite his problems and dependence on others, people would have to like him in order to want to help him. I think of the old adage that "We must always be careful not to bite the hand that feeds us." Somehow, many parents forget that a child who is physically challenged needs to be as well behaved as his physical, mental, or emotional problems allow. We do not want his behavior to get in the way of whatever love he could get from other people.

Mark is well-liked and frequently the most popular person in most situations; however, he did not get that way overnight. My wife and I have been criticized by his teachers and friends for being too strict and for disciplining him and holding him to the same standards of behavior we have for our other child. I, like my father and his father before him, became the heavy.

Providing discipline for a child with a disability is difficult: frequently, we are torn between letting him have his way or taking charge in certain matters. Visitors and relatives have a hard time understanding our need to discipline Mark. He can look so pitiful, sitting in his wheelchair, head down, crying. My wife and I are both from families that believe that firm but loving discipline is essential to raising responsible children. To deny Mark that same tradition would be a disservice to our son.

I feel it is important for men to be involved in the lives of boys with severe physical disabilities. My son sees so many ladies that I have to play a very pivotal role in his emotional growth and development. Yet there are pressures associated with this responsibility. There is no road map for how to be a "good father of a physically disabled child" and not many role models. There are also few to share the problems or the joys with. With my daughter, I remember many people wanting to strike up a conversation and discuss their children. I found that when I brought up Mark and his many challenges, other parents simply felt overwhelmed and changed the topic.

Over the years people have suggested many silly remedies to cure Mark of his disabilities. People would ask us if we were giving him enough iron or if we had tried old-time medicines. We had to learn tolerance and compassion for those well-meaning people. I missed not being able to call my mother to get child-rearing advice. We, instead, called medical specialists, and paid a fortune for it.

On occasion, I miss trading the "little man" tales told by fathers of eleven-year-old boys. These are stories fathers tell about their sons trying to be men and the conversation fathers have with their "little men." Most of these fathers, meaning to be kind, don't ask me about my little man.

There are moments when Mark tells me of his plans for the future. His perception of the future is wholesome and in line with that of other boys his age. He sometimes talks about the kind of car he wants to drive or about becoming a math teacher like his mom or a computer expert like his neighbor. There are no exceptions made for his disabilities or plans for altering his expectations to reflect the challenges of his circumstance. He dreams in color.

Mark has great aspirations for the future. I struggle with whether I should nurture these aspirations or should I attempt to temper them with what I see as realistic?

How can I tell an eleven-year-old how he should dream based on my perception of his potential? There are times when I wake up at two o'clock in the morning, trying to sort out this dilemma. Despite my soul-searching, I know there are no earthly answers to the question. Besides, who am I to tell an eleven-year-old that he has no right to dream?

There are certain realities that I know we have to confront. Among them is the fact that people often are so engrossed with the messenger that they never hear the message. Now that Mark is almost a teenager, his appearance has an impact on people. Many seem confounded by his appearance. On occasion Mark will roll up to people and start an intelligent, appropriate, and worthwhile conversation, yet the person he is talking to seems to only see the wheels on his chair. There was a time when he would simply go on talking. Now I notice that Mark is frustrated with these short-sighted people.

Next year, Mark will begin middle school and I fear the beginning of another round of battles with his educators. As we approach the end of the school year, I become apprehensive about next year. We have fought so many battles already. Now that I am older, I can see that some of the confrontations were necessary, but some were not. While it's important to pick your battles carefully, it can be hard to tell beforehand which are useful and which are not.

I suppose all parents worry about their children and their future. However, when you have a child who can't walk or feed himself the concerns are multiplied. With his teenage years approaching, it is becoming obvious that he will always be a very physically challenged person. I worry about his sister becoming too much of a protector of her "little brother." Over the years, she has become familiar with his entire medical history and current prognosis. We have tried not to burden her with any of his needs. I'll admit we have not discussed his future with her, although I know we need to.

I do not know what the future holds for my family. As a teacher and my family's leader, I feel driven to make this unnatural group succeed. I know that each day must be lived with a perspective that incorporates the past, the present, and the future. For my son's sake, I cannot afford the luxury of living for the moment. As necessary as I find this perspective, it is stressful and unnatural. When I was a child, my mother's measure of success for parenting was that, if you did it right, someone would be around to bring you a glass of water when you were old. I have to accept the reality of the fact that I will, as long as I live or how much I age, have someone to whom I must bring a glass of water. It is an unnatural state of affairs, one that I must continually adapt to.

If I were to offer advice to other fathers of children with disabilities, I would encourage them to be pragmatic. Realize that others will only understand part of your being and few will understand the road you must travel. Keep something for yourself—don't define your life in terms of your child. To do so will eat away at your health, both physical and mental. Appreciate that as a father, you have a unique perspective and put that perspective to good use.

Harrison Dixon is a vocational educator at Gloucester High School in Gloucester, Virginia. In addition to teaching, Harrison works with several community groups, including the local Special Education Advisory Committee. His interests outside family and work include teaching Sunday School, rose gardening, writing, and reading.

He Canters
When He Can

Greg Palmer

When Ned was four he began exhibiting some classic autistic behavior, which I'm told is rare for a child with Down syndrome. He would go off into a corner for hours and babble incoherently to himself, while slowly, rhythmically rocking his body. We were concerned, of course, but not unduly. Otherwise Ned was a very happy, outgoing boy who was making good intellectual and physical progress. He especially liked phonograph records and television, and would listen to and watch the same material over and over again. His ability to entertain himself for hours, whether by record, video tape, or his own internal, unintelligible monologues, was often a relief for us, a respite from the intense attention he otherwise needed.

A few years after the monologues began, he was rocking and talking one Sunday afternoon while I sat

reading the paper, not paying any attention to the meaningless recitation going on nearby. And I suddenly heard
him say, clearly, precisely, and with feeling, "You're a
very bad man. No, I'm a very good man, I'm just a very
bad wizard." He was reciting *The Wizard of Oz*. And I
had heard that one exchange between Dorothy and the
Wizard because Ned instinctively knew that it was the-
matically one of the most important bits of dialogue in
the film, so he'd given it a little extra in the performance. (That may be a father's fantasy, but I'm sticking
with it.)

When he got to "There's no place like home!" that
day, he started reciting the film again. He had memorized it, all of it, with appropriate sound effects. (His tor-
nado was particularly spectacular.) I soon learned he had
memorized all of the Disney *Snow White* too, as well as
a *Snow White* and *Puss In Boots* I had written and vide-
otaped for the Seattle Children's Theatre, most of the
television episodes of Jim Henson's *Muppet Babies,* and
the songs on a dozen different recordings by Raffi, Fred
Penner, Rosenschontz, and others. It occurred to me
that Ned had never been babbling incoherently, that all
those years he was entertaining himself with the material
he liked. I had underestimated him badly, and I've tried
never to do that again.

Ned is almost thirteen now, and he still talks to himself for long periods, But now the stories he tells are his
own stories, complex fantasies he creates and constantly
revises about knights, dragons, Ninja Turtles, volcanoes,
hot dogs, Mick Jagger, wizards, his pets, himself; all the
things he finds enthralling. Sitting and listening outside
the door when Ned is taking a bath is like listening to an
old radio show, back when there was still some creativity

in radio. Hundreds of characters wander through our bathroom two or three times a week, to do their turn on the stage in Ned's imagination and then wait in his memory for the next time.

Occasionally Ned will go off into his world in public, when we're waiting for a movie to start, or riding the ferry. I'll see people around us stare at him, then look away quickly, and their expressions will be of pity, "That poor boy," they are saying to themselves, "no mind at all, just babbling away like that. Too bad." They're making the same mistake I did, so I really shouldn't blame them; still, suppressing the desire to pass amongst such people with a baseball bat is one of the things I've had to work on as Ned's father.

I know how lucky I am that Ned is the way he is. And I don't mean because being the father of a developmentally disabled child has had a beneficial effect on me, has made me a more sensitive, caring, loving person. I hope it has, but whenever I hear other parents going on at length about the personal growth they have experienced as the caregiver for a special child, I want to—as I think Dorothy Parker once said—fwow up. Personal growth is valuable and necessary, an obvious and undeniable benefit of any parenting experience. But I've never thought my principal job as a father was to nurture and raise *me*. Recognizing how any situation has affected you is useful, but not if you become obsessive about those effects. Developmentally disabled children—all children, for that matter—are usually obsessive enough without parental role models.

I recently read a manuscript written by a man whose son also has Down syndrome. Page after page dripped with his new and unique opportunities to discover himself, get in touch with his inner person and, like, grow. He was having nothing but life-enhancing, spiritual experiences with his little Bobby. There was no mention of stubbornness, terrors in the night, constant respiratory problems, or the refusal to eat anything that isn't brown. Everything was just peachy for these two. And though actual information about Bobby was minimal—it was all Dad's catharsis-of-the-week stuff—I began to think this father was raising a remarkable, extremely high functioning child. I envied and admired him. And then halfway through the manuscript, in a chapter about all the things Dad was learning about himself during toilet training, he mentioned offhand that Bobby is a non-reading, mostly non-verbal twelve-year-old who can neither feed nor dress himself.

I feel sorry for that father, and especially sorry for his son. Bobby doesn't have many obvious victories for them to enjoy together, so Dad has turned to his own spiritual awakening for enjoyment and consolation. Emotionally he seems to be living off his own accomplishments, as I'm sure he once dreamed of living off his son's. And though it would be grossly presumptuous of me to contend that Bobby is as low-functioning as he is because his father had become so self-obsessed, I think it is at least a possibility. Dad has used Bobby as an opportunity and an excuse to turn into himself. Ironically, by doing so he may have turned away from his son, the person he loves, but also the person who spoiled his dreams of the future and frightens him now.

I never consciously tried to avoid the pitfalls of parental self-aggrandizement because originally I didn't know they existed. I think I was blindly lucky in a choice I made. From the day our pediatrician called and said the genetic test was positive, I've tried to approach Ned's situation as logically, rationally, and realistically as possible. Part of that was concentrating on his immediate and long-range needs, and not on my own fears—or my ego.

I remember sitting on my front porch that sweet September evening when we first learned that Ned had Down syndrome, and suddenly having the chilling realization that, not for as long as *we* lived, but for as long as *he* lived, Ned would be our responsibility; not the state's, not his relatives', especially not his brother's. We could hope that some day Ned would be self-sufficient, and work as hard as possible with him towards that goal. We could trust that his older brother would take care of him in their adulthood, not because he had to, but because he wanted to. But we still had to be prepared for the physical, financial, emotional alternative—parental custody, even from beyond the grave. Loving Ned with all our hearts would never be enough.

That preparation, both of Ned and his world to be, has taken planning, patience, and research, including knowing what opportunities are available within the community. Ned was three weeks old when he went to his first infant stimulation class at the University of Washington's Experimental Education Unit. That was just the beginning of a quest for good schools, camps, and experiences, a quest that will never end.

Even so, I've found the essence of raising a special child is not in the grand questions, not in the philosophical discussion of the concept of private property in modern society, for instance, but the more immediate question of "What did you do with my watch?" While not losing sight of the big picture, it is the daily business of life, the million things we do at home with and for Ned, that seem to have the most beneficial effect on him, and us.

Just one example. I can't recall a time when Cathy or I haven't read to him in the evening right before he goes to bed, beginning with the simplest *Spot The Dog* and *Curious George* books when he was an infant, clear through to yesterday evening, when he and I read the newspaper together (Ned especially likes disaster news), another chapter of Beverly Cleary's *Henry and Beezus,* plus four or five poems. And the effect of that reading has been both general—contributing to Ned's unique imagination and dramatic flair—and specific. When he wakes us in the middle of the night now, sometimes he calls for us, but most often he picks up the book he's working on by himself, reads for a while, and then goes back to sleep.

His current interest is biographies—Jefferson, Washington, Lincoln, especially Martin Luther King Jr. For ten Halloweens in a row Ned was the same witch, but this past year he finally wanted to be someone else. He wanted to be the Reverend Dr. King, as a tribute to a man he's read about and admires. It was a wonderful idea and we were proud of him, even if we didn't have the slightest idea how we were going to turn this little white kid into his hero without offending half the neighborhood, makeup-wise. (We decided on just a dark suit and glasses. To me Ned looked more like Roy Orbison than Martin Luther King, but he was satisfied.) As his father, I know the memory of this past Halloween and the Martin Luther King Dilemma will eventually overwhelm any memories of a decade of trying to talk a very stubborn little boy out of that ratty witch costume.

I'm making Ned sound like the perfect kid, a constant delight to everyone all the time. That is not my intention, and not the case. Just as dangerous as concentrating on your personal growth to the exclusion of your child, is convincing yourself that there's nothing all that different about a child with special needs, thereby ignoring or repressing the challenges, and the behavior, that is part of why the child is special in the first place. Both are ways to escape reality, and I've tried, less successfully I suspect, to avoid the latter as much as the former.

Somebody must say it. Developmentally disabled children can be a real pain in the butt, and there is no guilt in a parent admitting that to him or herself, any more than a parent should feel guilty because a "normal" teenager still leaves his dirty socks around. As his father I make allowances for Ned, because he is special, that I would not make were he just a typically tedious pre-teen.

His diet, for instance. Ned eats: wieners, which he peels; white toast without crusts; cheeseburgers as long as there are no sesame seeds on the outside of the buns and only ketchup, mustard, meat, and cheese on the inside; vanilla ice cream out of cones which he then discards; cheese pizza; Chips Ahoy cookies; milk and Coke; dry Cheerios; and absolutely nothing else. He doesn't even eat candy, or any other kind of cookie, breakfast cereal, or ice cream. And this has been going on for years. (Imagine the smell of a microwaved wiener, dripping with grease, at 6 a.m. Tuesday morning. Now imagine it for 2000 mornings in a row.) Ned's stubbornness about food makes long trips, restaurant visits, overnight stays and meals at the homes of friends a recurring hassle. But we put up with it, because he is Ned. And if, between the wieners and Cheerios, we can occasionally get him to nibble on some broccoli, or just try Grandma's manicotti, then it's a victory. We can go on dreaming that some morning he'll come downstairs and casually ask for a vegetarian omelet and a tankard of grapefruit juice.

For all his occasional obstinacy, though, the hardest thing about being Ned's father is contemplating the future. I want no more and no less than for Ned to be happy every day of his life. But I judge happiness on my terms, from my experience. Happiness for me is being married for 26 years to a woman I love, and having children I love as well. Happiness is having good and talented friends, interesting work to do, and the freedom to stop doing it for a while and just go somewhere. And Ned may never have any of these things.

I did a news story once about two wonderful people who are, as far as I know, the only Down syndrome married couple in America. So I know there is a chance that some day Ned will find a person to love and cherish, who will love and cherish him as much as we do now. But at best it's unlikely. Children of his own are impossible. He will probably never drive a car, never wander around Europe with a backpack and a friend or two, never have a job where he can say he made a difference in anyone's life but his own. The principal disadvantage of that decision always to deal with Ned's situation logically and realistically is that I can't shake it, even when I want to, even when I want to fantasize about a glorious future for him.

But that's a lot different than giving up. Only my own narrowness of vision makes me think that when

Ned's 46, his idea of happiness will be what mine is now. And if there is some overlap, I know his mother and I have done all we can to get him ready. If he wants to wander around Europe when he's 20, at least he's known the countries he'll be able to visit since he was ten.

He will be a very good man, and maybe a very good wizard.

Greg Palmer has been writing professionally since 1968, principally for broadcast. His most recent project was as producer/writer/host of a PBS documentary series, "Death: The Trip of a Lifetime," which concerned how cultures around the world face life's end. The series first aired in October 1993, when Mr. Palmer's book of the series was published by HarperCollins. Greg has been the film and theater critic for Seattle's KING Television and a "signature" reporter for both NBC and CBS affiliates, winning 13 Emmy awards, the Peabody, and other honors. He is currently in pre-production on a PBS series about vaudeville, to be broadcast in 1995. Greg has also written seven plays for families that have been published and produced internationally. His last theatrical work, "The Magic Apple," was written in collaboration with Ned Palmer and based on his story of a prince, a dragon, and a wizard.

Heroes Come In All Shapes

―――――――――――――

Robley K. Yee

Heroes come in all shapes and sizes. Some prove their courage on fields of battle and others stand alone against the rush of the crowds. This is a story of a quiet boy who must live in a world that is often bewildering and full of danger and of his parents who must aid in the negotiation with that world. But, if the truth be told, it is about a young man who continues to teach his father of the complexities and value of daily life.

My son, Matthew, entered his teen years last summer and fully relishes being thirteen. He continues to proudly remind us and his younger sister, to her distress, of his age. With each reminder we are advised that being a teenager brings with it some unseen privileges or some mythical status unknowable to those who have already passed through, like parents and other adults, and of course excluding those who have not passed that marker, like younger sisters. I must admit being in my mid-forties and my memories of that age are fading into comfortable narratives that in a few years will become great personal myths unrecognizable to even those who experienced them with me.

So how does a mortal like me, a father of two children, share what little I know with my teenage son? It was so much easier when I could take him by the hand and walk him across the street or excite him with a small bag of chips. Now, I not only must let him cross the street alone, but begin to internally let him go as he handles the multitude of details that make up his everyday responsibilities. It was so much simpler when social relationships mainly centered on the family, but now friendships with others his age have become more important.

Then, of course, there is the topic of romance and sexuality. Whenever I gather the courage to approach the subject with Matthew I intend to appear fatherly with an aura of worldliness, but all the while I feel more like someone learning to ballroom dance in combat boots.

I have consulted with Nancy about counseling Matthew on these topics. My wife of twenty-plus years, Nancy, can handle multiple tasks simultaneously and keeps us all going in the proper direction. But, on this topic, she has no pearls of wisdom to share. She shrugs her shoulders and quietly walks out of the room, muttering something about it's a father's duty. My colleagues at work are a bit more supportive, but seem somewhat cavalier. I get the impression that I should just proceed as if it was a simple task. Besides, it is the natural obligation of being a dad.

So, what is a father to do? The world is full of intricate events and social interactions that require sophisticated responses. It is not a uniformly benevolent world, but a world where some errors can lead to painful personal consequences, whether emotional (personal rejection, ridicule, and loneliness) or physical (gunshot wounds, AIDS).

Yet, I realize that it would be impossible and ill-advised to attempt to protect Matthew from all forms of distress. This is my dilemma: when to hold on to him and what to let him experience. It is a conflict that all parents, I suspect, must in one form or another grapple with and in so doing, give meaning to our lives. However, the dilemma may be particularly difficult for those who have children with some form of disability.

Each society has some general norms of conduct and individuals in that society must conform to these rules. Development of sexuality is multi-dimensional and "learning the rules" of sexual and interpersonal conduct results from integrating a myriad of frequently competing personal and societal phenomena and processes. These can include: sexual urges, social proscriptions, interpersonal attraction, personal security, physical changes, knowledge of one's limitations, and the capacity to view others as sexual beings who have their own needs, desires, and rights.

As talk shows and best-selling books attest, successful integration of these processes and phenomena is difficult enough for those who do not face intellectual challenges. But what of those who do?

The importance of placing sexuality in the context of significant relationships is a value I prize and would like to uphold and pass on to my children. Thus, it is at

this point that my latest parental "trial" arises. Matthew
finds it difficult to exert his wishes in social relationships
so others can respond reciprocally. Sometimes he will
act in silly or provocative ways to secure attention; other
times he will withdraw and observe or have others do
for him. All these methods allow him to function at
some level in social settings, but clearly they are not desirable as he tries to develop and negotiate healthy interpersonal relationships.

Matthew has a teenager's desire to have meaningful
platonic and romantic relationships with others; yet he
currently lacks the skills to create them. In my efforts to
help my son navigate these murky waters, I find that I
have no easy solutions to offer my son. However, I do
employ several strategies that have been helpful.

First, I try as best I can to see the world from Matthew's point of view. For Matthew, the world can often
be a bewildering place; to help him, I need to understand the world as he sees it. Second, I try to listen to his
concerns, and listen as nonjudgementally as possible.
(This can be difficult. Although Matthew has much to
say, actually saying it is difficult: It can take Matthew ten
minutes to say what his sister can say in 30 seconds. To
be available to my son, I find I must shut up and listen.)
Third, despite my desire to know and understand Matthew, I have come to accept that I cannot ever know him
completely. He will always have qualities, desires, interests, and motivations that I will never fully understand.
To pretend to know him fully would be a violation of
who he is, his very personhood.

Each time I use these strategies, I find that I learn
from Matthew a little more about his world and he of
mine. But, I must admit that in my attempts to teach

Matthew about sexuality, relationships, and life, he has already taught me more than I can ever teach him. Since the time of his birth and diagnosis at 9 months, Matthew has challenged me to justify my views of the world, beliefs, and even simple, everyday activities. Because he has taught me that life can be tenuous—and therefore a greater gift—I must account for my purpose.

I don't want to over-intellectualize what we as a family experienced since we learned of Matthew's disability: there has been much grief and frustration. However, as I ponder my relationship with my son, I frequently ask myself who is the mentor and who shows the greater courage? Can I do any less than what the world is asking of him?

Rob Yee lives in Seattle with Nancy, his wife of 24 years, a son, Matthew, a daughter, Megan, and a gerbil. Currently, Rob is enrolled as a doctoral student at the Fielding Institute and works as a probation counselor. He was born and raised in Honolulu and moved to Seattle in 1973 after graduating with a Master in Social Work from the University of Hawaii. The Yees feel fortunate to have a circle of extended family members and friends who have provided support and kindness throughout the many trials that Rob and Nancy have experienced as parents of a child with special needs.

Best Friends

James C. Wilson

My 13–year-old son Sam wants to leave early for
Family Night at his school. This year, as an extra attraction, the PTA has added a karaoke show to the annual
spaghetti dinner, and Sam wants to check it out. So
we're among the first to arrive in the school cafeteria,
decked out in blue and white tablecloths. The teachers,
parents, and cafeteria workers all say hello to Sam. Sam
pretends not to notice, but my wife and I see the big
smile on his face as he carries his tray over to one of the
lunch tables and begins eating his chocolate cupcake
first. Everyone knows Sam.

By the time we finish our dinner, the people from
Sound Productions have set up their karaoke machine
on the stage in the rear of the cafeteria. Speakers, stand-
up microphone, and video prompter, all tested and
ready for action.

When one of the workers comes to our table distributing lists of songs available, Sam asks, "Do we have to sing?" The man laughs and says, "Only if you want to."

Sam ignores him, scouring the song titles for some of his favorites. No R.E.M., but he does find the Beatles and Willie Nelson. Close enough.

Meanwhile, the karaoke people do all the work. They take turns singing on stage, everything from Garth Brooks to Johnny Mathis. Still no requests from the audience, a subdued crowd of curious but shy kids, accompanied by parents who huddle over their plates pretending to be invisible.

But not Sam. He finds a song he likes, "Georgia on My Mind," and asks us to write it down on a slip of paper. My wife, gritting her teeth, takes the note up to the stage.

"Hey—here's a request," the speakers blare. "From Sam Wilson. He wants to hear 'Georgia on My Mind.' Do you want to sing it, Sam?"

And before we can blink an eye, our eager 13-year-old takes off. He rambles awkwardly through the maze of tables, exactly as he would walk to his classroom or anywhere else. Maybe he has to be helped up on stage, but no matter. When he gets that microphone in his hands and the music kicks in, there's Sam rocking from side to side, crooning out the words to "Georgia on My Mind." A jazz version, a la Ray Charles, with a few extra howls and screams thrown in for effect. He doesn't miss a beat.

The karaoke people can't believe the performance. Neither can the audience. The parents give Sam a big hand as he finishes the song and starts hamming it up for everyone to see, doing a few dance steps for his encore.

After Sam breaks the ice, other kids rush to the stage wanting to sing. And Sam? He's off looking for something else to do.

"Sam, that was great!" the assistant principal tells him on his way out of the cafeteria. "I'm going to tell your teacher tomorrow morning."

"Okay," he says over his shoulder. And then he's gone, the Karaoke Kid.

Moments like these remind me of the miracle of Sam's development. I've taken nothing for granted since the day Sam was born with congenital hydrocephalus, his head size 47 centimeters (compared to a mean of 35 in "normal" newborns). Two days later Sam was shunted with a VP shunt that drains excess cerebrospinal fluid from his brain down into his abdomen. Like many infants with shunts, Sam required multiple shunt revisions during the first three years of his life, years that exhausted my wife and me both physically and emotionally. Having a strong relationship helped us get through that difficult period. So, too, did Sam, who was and still is the source of our strength. He fought so hard. How could we do any less?

Since his third birthday Sam has needed only two shunt revisions and has remained relatively free of other medical problems. Still, Sam has a variety of disabilities and autistic-like behaviors caused by his enlarged, malformed ventricles. For example, he has visual problems (including no depth perception) and fine motor delays (including an inability to write). Sam has poor balance and an ambling gate that makes him appear clumsier than he really is. Also, he tends to be hyperactive, rocking from side to side and chattering nonstop about everything from school buses to tornadoes.

"A miracle," Sam's neurosurgeon remarked on our last visit to his office. The kid born with only a "thin layer of brain tissue," according to the report from his first CT-scan, now goes to junior high, mainstreamed except for his home room assignment. For home room Sam uses the Learning Resource Center, where he has his own computer and work space. Over the years Sam's IQ has climbed from 62 to 113 as measured by the cognitive ability tests administered by school psychologists for his yearly placement reevaluations. His development has been remarkable, thanks to the love and hard work of his teachers and family. And thanks to Sam, who's worked hardest of all.

Sometimes I find it difficult to tell him exactly how I feel. As a teenager he's beginning to assert his independence, rebelling in his funny unique way against parental authority. Rebelling, especially, against his father. Yet he knows that I'm prouder of being his father than anything else I've ever done. More than my career, more than the books I've written, Sam is my life's work.

Fathering Sam puts everything else in perspective. Not that it's been easy. My wife and I have both made sacrifices in our careers, a fact that many of our colleagues can't or won't understand. Different people, different priorities. But no matter. Our commitment to Sam has helped us sort out what we value most.

Sam and I spend lots of time together. During the school year there's not much time for recreation, except on the weekends. After school I'm usually waiting for him when his big yellow school bus pulls up in front of our house. No way I can miss seeing my son bouncing up and down on the seat behind the driver, talking 90 miles an hour to whoever's sitting next to him. When the door swings open, he cocks his head back to look for me, squinting through his glasses. Only when he sees me waiting in the driveway does he collect his belongings, searching the seat and the floor in front of him for his baseball cap, jacket, and backpack. And when he steps down, holding on to the door handle and feeling with his left foot, his face breaks out in a smile. And something else, a sense of accomplishment.

"I had a good day!" he says, triumphantly.

Or:

"I had an okay day . . . but it could have been worse!" Which tells me I'd better look for the teacher's note inside his back pack.

Once he gets home Sam loves the routine he's established over the years. First comes homework, which usually turns into a struggle between parents and teenager, a test of wills. After he finishes his work and I finish pulling out my hair, he reads his newspaper, sometimes a local newspaper but most often USA TODAY, because he loves the detail and the color on the weather page. Then he watches television. Not cartoons or soap operas. Not Sam, he watches the local news, followed by a half hour or so of the Weather Channel. Only then does it occur to him to report for dinner.

On weekends Sam and I go to movies, sometimes just the two of us, and sometimes with his friends. Not all kids feel comfortable with Sam or are willing to put up with his incessant questions about school and weather, but those who do quickly become valued friends. "Buds," Sam calls them, borrowing a term from *Wayne's World,* one of his favorite movies.

Sam has his own distinct personality, his own likes and dislikes that set him apart from most kids his age.

He's not interested in sports, except for swimming and on occasion riding his bicycle with the extra large training wheels for balance. Every so often he'll agree to go for a hike, but mostly to stop me from pestering him about "exercise," a dreaded word in Sam's vocabulary. He hates amusement parks and shopping malls, mostly because he's distracted by the noise and the crowds. But also, I suspect, because he really doesn't understand how people can enjoy going on scary rides or spending money at the malls. The consumer lifestyle will never be Sam's. Which doesn't bother me one bit.

Sam takes pleasure in other activities. He loves to read, everything from weather books and encyclopedias to *Parents Magazine* and young adult novels. But his favorite is *Weatherwise Magazine,* which comes out bimonthly, a terrible disappointment to Sam, who wishes it would come out biweekly. He's always on the phone, calling the neighborhood bookstore that sells the magazine, wanting to know when the next issue will arrive. "Hot off the presses," he'll say.

And Sam loves music. Teenage music, he likes to point out. He listens to R.E.M., Bruce Springsteen, and his favorite radio stations, all of them blasting a motley assortment of pseudo-music that drives his parents crazy. "I'm a teenager, what do you expect?" he asks.

When he was younger, Sam would listen to the music of Bob Dylan and Neil Young and play his harmonica along with them. "What happened to the good old days?" I asked him recently. Meaning, of course, the days when he listened to music I like.

"Gone!" he said, waving a thumb over his shoulder, as an umpire does when ejecting a player from a baseball game. "Out of here!"

Sam feels proud to be a 13–year-old. "Did you ever think I would come this far?" he often asks, knowing full well that his development has surprised and delighted everyone. He tries his best to be cool, cocking his baseball cap at weird angles and insisting on taking a bath every morning so he can be clean "for the girls." But sometimes his definition of cool seems a bit eccentric, such as when he rubs underarm deodorant on the side of his face. No doubt about it, Sam marches to a different drummer.

Sam's teachers tell us wonderful stories about what a charmer he can be. Not infrequently he will breeze into a classroom and remark to one especially mature teenage girl, "You look lovely today!"

Some of the stories are hard to believe. My 13–year-old said that? Sam?

Not that raising Sam is always fun and games. I don't want to underestimate the hard work involved. Sam gets frustrated easily, so that even the simplest task, like putting on his socks, can become a problem if he's in an impatient mood. Too, he's distracted by crowds of people and loud noises, especially sirens. For that reason he hates ambulances and fire trucks. Sometimes even an object being out of place on a table or in a room can make it impossible for Sam to concentrate. And since he has little feeling in his fingers, he sometimes doesn't realize how hard he's pinching or grabbing someone, a cause for concern both at school and at home. He's been sent to the principal's office on a couple of occasions for pinching or grabbing one of his classmates. For losing his cool, as he puts it.

Still, these setbacks seem minor for a kid who's come so far. Even his teachers agree, telling us poignant stories about how after one of these incidents Sam will confess his guilt and apologize profusely. Or, conversely, how he will put on a stubborn face and proclaim, "No, I'm not sorry!"

Disciplining Sam can be maddening, because he can go from charming to stubborn and back again all in the same breath. Though his willfulness sometimes makes me angry, this same willfulness has enabled him to overcome many of his disabilities. Because of Sam, I've come to understand the power of the human will, the desire not simply to survive, but to grow and develop. To become whatever one can.

Summers tend to be more relaxing because Sam doesn't have to worry about school or homework. He can "party," as he likes to boast. He swims most every day, and in the early part of the summer he plays T-Ball in the neighborhood Challenger Little League. Except Sam's version of T-Ball differs from that of his teammates. Sam plays a talking game. He whacks the ball, then trots around the bases asking the puzzled members of the opposing team questions about the weather. Much the same happens when Sam's team, the mighty Lakota Cubs, takes the field. Usually Sam can't be bothered with the balls that come his way. If he does decide to field a ball, it's because he wants to throw or carry it to a particular teammate so that the two of them can chat about, you guessed it, the weather. For Sam, baseball's just another form of conversation.

Sam takes certain aspects of the game seriously, though. For example, he looks forward to lining up after the final out and giving everyone high-fives. Even better are the soft drinks and other treats the parents pass out after the game. And nicknames, Sam loves nicknames.

His have changed over the years, from Slammin' Sam to Stormin' Sam to, most recently, Moose. Why Moose? Not because of the way he plays baseball, though some might find resemblance there, but because of the Mangy Moose Saloon cap be bought one summer in Jackson Hole, Wyoming. Since then he's moved on to other baseball caps, but for some reason the nickname stuck. Moose.

For many years I didn't dare to think about the future. In truth, the future seemed impossible. Today it doesn't, even though I still can't answer many of the big questions. Will Sam be able to live independently? Will he be able to have a job and provide, at least partially, for his own needs? Will he be able to go to college?

One thing I do know, however. Sam has an enormous capacity to enjoy life. Given a quiet, structured environment, Sam can live a happy and productive life—on his own terms. My greatest desire is to give him this opportunity. It's what I meant earlier when I said Sam was my life's work. I owe him this, because he's already given me as much love and happiness as I will ever be able to give him. Without Sam I would never have realized what it truly means to be a father.

"Dad, will we always be best friends?" Sam asked me the other day.

"Absolutely," I said. "Absolutely."

In addition to maintaining a household and fathering a teenager turned amateur meteorologist, James C. Wilson teaches in the Writing Program at the University of Cincinnati, where he is an associate professor. His books include John Reed for the Masses *(1987) and, most recently,* The Hawthorne and Melville Friendship

(1991). He also writes fiction and nonfiction when time allows, and his creative work has appeared in a number of literary reviews. James and his family have lived in the Cincinnati area for eleven years; before that they lived in Albuquerque, New Mexico, where Sam was born in 1980.

Loving from Afar

Larry Searcy

As the phone clicked dead I had an uneasy feeling. Aaron had seemed uninvolved, distant, maybe even cold. It had been several weeks since we had had a conversation that felt warm and spontaneous. I hadn't heard him laugh during most of that time. My mind went into overdrive. Was he losing interest in talking to me? Was our "long distance" relationship simply no longer important to him? Or was his coldness attributable to something else in his life totally unconnected with me? The silence on the other end of the phone held no answers.

It hadn't always been like this. Before the separation and eventual divorce, Aaron and I were practically inseparable. When Aaron was first diagnosed with a severe hearing loss, I grieved over the fact that he wouldn't hear music or birds singing or even my voice as others do. So a few years later, when the second diagnosis of Fasciocapulohumeral (FSH) dystrophy came in, I felt I was somewhat prepared for it and took on the attitude

that, by God, whatever Aaron wanted to do in life, he
would do! I would see to it!

If Aaron wanted to play baseball, I was there working with the league and team coach to show them simple
accommodations that would allow Aaron to be on the
team with his friends. We never missed a practice or a
game.

I'll never forget the first game of Aaron's one-sea-
son baseball career. The coach, well meaning though he
was, truly wanted his team to win. In spite of Aaron's hit-
ting ability which he had witnessed in practice, the coach
cut a deal with the other team that Aaron's at-bats simply wouldn't count. The first time Aaron came to bat
there were runners on second and third. Aaron hit the
ball out of the infield, both runners scored and Aaron's
pinch-runner ended up on second base. The opposing
coach immediately stopped the game and insisted that
the runners return to their bases because Aaron's at-bats
didn't count. By the next game, Aaron's at-bats counted.
In spite of his FHS muscular dystrophy, Aaron was a
team leader. He led through his daily display of courage.
His friends innately recognized his efforts and respected
him for who he was . . . and I was there through it all. It
was a victory for Aaron and for me.

I was there for Cub Scouts, camping trips, fishing
excursions, and all of the things boys do during their elementary school years. In short, my relationship with
Aaron was anchored on day-to-day, close and intense
contact. He let me serve as his legs and on occasion, his
travel expediter. He also taught me about courage, unsel-
fish caring about others, and boundless determination.
We were father and son, friends and running mates.
There was nothing, I believed, that I would not do to as-

sure that he realized his full potential and get the most out of life.

Approximately four years ago that all changed. At about that time a series of life-altering events forced me to face my marriage in the context of an unvarnished reality I had long avoided. After hours of counseling and introspection I now suspect that my marriage had been in trouble from the beginning. I had simply been too busy to notice. As I look back over those years, it is increasingly clear that Aaron and his sister Kate were the glue that held the marriage together for roughly ten years longer than it might have otherwise lasted.

The fight to gain services for Aaron, however, was especially bonding. There was always a common foe at which to direct energy and emotion. My ex-wife and I could attribute our lack of emotion for each other to the fatigue of the "good fight." And the fight was never-ending. We took on all comers: doctors, educators, Scout officials, recreation directors, neighbors, and others. We either won or the fight wasn't over. If we didn't get what Aaron needed, the fat lady never sang.

My image of the world and of myself was shaped and molded through the cumulative trials, tribulations, and successes of our fight for Aaron's place in the sun. Through all of this I am ashamed to admit that I developed a sense of unspoken superiority over other parents of children with disabilities who didn't fight the good fight. I understood the pain they went through but I couldn't understand why they too weren't laying themselves on the line as I was. As part and parcel of this inflated vision of myself, I never saw a fight I couldn't win. I was self-sacrificing and was the embodiment of a great parent. I lived for my kid. I sacrificed for my kid. And I did it all with the panache of a happy warrior.

But in the end, it wasn't enough. I couldn't survive my life as it was. I had to let go of my marriage if I was to survive. In doing so, I also had to let go of my relationship with Aaron as he and I had lived it and we had to develop a new way of relating to each other.

I didn't give up easily however. I fought for the physical custody of both Aaron and his sister, but was defeated in court. Since that time Aaron has lived with his mother, approximately 1,200 miles away from me. Kate lives with me.

Aaron and I spend time together on holidays and summers. Hence, our primary mode of communication is by telephone. I try to "reach out and touch" Aaron at least every other day and often, every day. But now when small or significant things happen in Aaron's life, I'm not there.

When we were together, I brought to Aaron an expectation that he would behave and mature like anyone else. We battled over homework, chores, and all manner of things that all parents must work through with their children. Now I find that day-to-day discipline, while important, is out of my field of influence. I still ask about homework each day and urge him to get it done, but we both know that I can't really influence his actions as I used to.

Our relationship has changed. He has as much control over it as I do. Maybe more. He can decide if he wants to talk to me, about what and for how long. He can tell me only what he wants me to know and I'm no wiser. He can express any opinion he wishes with little or no consequences.

In a strange sort of way this leveling of control has been good for us. I have come to know Aaron unfettered by the politics of day-to-day living. He tells me about adventures, for instance, that he stresses he does not want his mother to know about. Like all children separated from their parents, he is struggling to shake off the shackles of a parent/child relationship and establish himself as an independent, unique person. Like all parents, I am pleased to see him grow but I find myself clinging to the relationship we once had and wishing that it could go on forever. Most parents face this phenomenon about the time their child goes off to college or takes up other endeavors outside of the family home. Aaron and I started much earlier.

I have also had to adjust my image of myself. This adjustment has not been easy. At first, in an unconscious effort to make up for being absent and possibly to bribe him into living with me , I tried to make our time together a wall-to-wall extravaganza. We partied down all day, every day. Nothing was too good for my son. Cost be damned. Over time, however, Aaron has helped me to realize that he didn't need or want a wall-to-wall party. He simply wanted time to be with me. He wanted a chance to do simple things together. Now we make the most of our time together by enjoying the mundane life rhythms and activities that most fathers and sons take for granted.

I've become reconciled to the notion that I will miss much of Aaron's life from here on out. The pain that once accompanied absence or separation from him has dulled a bit and has mingled with the pain all parents of children with disabilities carry with them. As time has passed and my life has begun to fall back into place, I linger less on my separation from Aaron and more on taking full advantage of the time we have together. Aaron showed me the way.

One night, during a phone conversation, Aaron asked me how I was doing. I replied that I was getting by but that I was saddened by the fact that I wouldn't see him for several months. Aaron sighed and very deliberately, and with great patience told me that I must "quit worrying about things you can't do and work at making the things you can do be the best they can be." That's the way Aaron lives each day of his life. I've tried to do that the same ever since.

My life situation has forced me to face the fact that apparently there are things I cannot—or will not—do for my son. The recognition that there are circumstances I cannot overcome or live with has been difficult to accept. I was, after all, a happy warrior who never accepted defeat where Aaron was concerned. Hence, I had to cope not only with the sense of failure that accompanies the early stages of all divorces, I also had to deal with the added guilt that I was failing Aaron. Of all of the pain of the divorce this feeling of failing my children—especially Aaron—was the worst.

Now I'm mostly over that. In spite of my absence, Aaron continues to live a good life. He has entered his teens. He has an interest in girls, ice hockey, video games, and comic books. He has a buddy in his neighborhood with whom he "hangs out." He's making the best of controlling what he can control and not worrying about what he cannot control.

I still harbor hopes that one day Aaron will decide to live with me. I realize, however, that as each day passes the likelihood becomes more and more remote.

But like Aaron, I am trying to do the best I can with the situation in which I live. In spite of great distance, Aaron and I are maintaining our relationship.

Based on the reporting of friends and colleagues, Aaron and I talk . . . *really talk,* more frequently and about a wider range of issues than many parents do with their teenage sons. The distance that separates us has, I think, stripped our relationship of a lot of the day-to-day details that sometimes cloud truly important things like feelings, honesty, and candor.

The relationship I have with Aaron can be simultaneously satisfying, gut wrenching, joyful, and depressing. Conversation cannot replace *being* together. Honest conversation, however, is better that the half-truths or surface conversation that infest some parent/child relationships. We are getting better at utilizing every moment we have together to really be together. We laugh and talk about "man stuff" like mustaches, sports, movies, and life.

Aaron and I are still getting used to not being together. He's handling it better than I. Loving from afar is not easy but it's something that most parents eventually have to face. It's hard work, but parents of children with disabilities are used to hard work, and as always, through it all, my son is teaching me about what in life really matters.

Larry Searcy has been Director of Programs and Government Relations for the National Parent Network on Disabilities since 1991. He is also President of Searcy and Associates, which provides consultation on organizational communication, consumer empowerment, and project management. Larry lives in Rockville, Maryland, and

*has community interests that include child abuse, assis-
tive technology, and homelessness.*

A Mosaic

———✦———

Bill Dodds

I considered using the image of a jigsaw puzzle but
that isn't right. The pieces don't fit together snugly. No,
life with Tom is more like a mosaic. Incidents. Memories. Fears. Celebrations. Successes. Pains. Questions. No
one part shows it all but if the viewer takes a step back, a
picture begins to emerge.

* * *

I come charging into my 18–year-old son's room.
Now I can't remember why. Probably to tell him to do
something.

Take out the garbage. Finish his homework. Get his
junk out of the living room.

He's on the phone. "So will you go out with me?"
he asks softly.

I slip back out, remembering how hard it is to ask a
girl for a date. How hard it is when she says no.

He comes out a little later. I can tell by his face what her answer was.

"Girls," I say and shake my head.

He shrugs.

* * *

An official government notice had come in the mail but we've lost it. Tom has to register for the Selective Service. No matter that he has been in special education all his school years. No matter that he has been classified mildly mentally retarded.

I'm not sure what Freud would make of it, but his mother Monica and I—children of the Vietnam protest era—have misplaced the information.

I end up calling all over trying to get some government worker to tell me what we have to do to get Tom registered. Finally, I find out we just need to go to our local post office.

I tell that to Tom one evening at dinner.

"I already signed that junk," he says. "At school."

What!

We check with his counselor and find out he's right. A few weeks later his paperwork—his draft card—comes in the mail. "Thomas Willum Dodds" it reads.

He doesn't know how to spell "William."

I correct it and send it back. The second one comes about a month after that.

* * *

Kids Tom's age are taking part in a Confirmation class at our Catholic parish. His mom and I aren't sure he can handle it and so we talk it over with the youth minister. She's very receptive.

Several months later Tom is standing up in front of the other kids, their parents, the youth minister, and the pastor. He's giving an oral report on a church he has visited. He's reading what he has written earlier that week.

It's one of the best of the evening.

I'm biased, of course.

But it is.

* * *

There's a call from the school early one morning. Did we know Tom was changing his clothes once he got there? That he was looking like a gang member?

Tom was our foster son before we adopted him when he was 14 months old. He was only two days old when Monica and I picked him up at the hospital. We are white; he is biracial, black and white. We have encouraged him to be proud of his heritage.

From the time he and his younger sister and brother were tots, we have repeated "No sex. No drugs. No alcohol. No cigarettes." We have warned them about cults and about molesters.

But there were no gangs in our suburban town then. Now there are. Now some members attend the local high school.

That morning we rush over to the school. His first period teacher has kept him in the classroom. We walk in and see he has different pants, a different shirt. A big coat. Someone else's shoes and hat.

Half an hour later his mom and I are so relieved. A gang member? He wasn't trying to dress like a gang member. He didn't realize that he was being groomed by a kid who, if not in a gang, is a wannabe. He didn't realize that someone who *is* in a gang could easily misinterpret the signals his borrowed clothes were sending.

No, he just didn't want to dress like a dork anymore. He didn't want to dress like . . . his father.

Tom and Monica go shopping that afternoon. He gets an assortment of new clothes, including a pair of baggy pants that sag in the back.

I can't help but mention that mine have done the same for years.

* * *

Out of the blue I call a former co-worker I haven't talked to since the late 1970s. We visit for a while and she asks about the kids.

I tell her Tom is doing well in his special education classes. He's going to be graduating from high school.

Oh?

He was just a toddler back then. She says she didn't know he had any learning problems.

I try to remember the time before we knew Tom had special needs.

I can't.

* * *

His school counselor sets up a meeting with us and a case manager from the state's Department of Vocational Rehabilitation.

Tom will be done with school in June. He could have stayed until he is 21 but he says he has had enough and his mother and I agree. Now we need to talk about what type of job he is interested in.

"Job?" he asks at the meeting.

"Training and a job," the case manager said.

"You don't just sit home and watch TV if you're not going to school," I tell him. "You go to work." Monica and his school counselor nod.

"Only till you're 65," I tease him. "Then you can re-tire."

He stares at me.

* * *

Monica and I don't know when we are dealing with a mentally retarded teen and when we are dealing with a normally rebelling teen. In any case, the house rules have begun to chafe. Tom doesn't see why he has to follow any.

"I'm 18," he insists. "I'm an adult. You can't tell me what to do anymore."

We give him the standard "As long as you're living in our house . . ."

Later I jot down a list in black felt-tip pen and tape it to the wall at the foot of his bed.

1. Diploma
2. Training
3. Job
4. Money
Apartment
Fun, Fun, Fun.

* * *

An image comes to mind. Tom has been going to school since he was 3. His teachers, his counselors and his mother and I have been pushing and pulling him up this hill.

He has come a long way.

Such a long way.

We are all so proud of him.

But now public school is ending. We've reached the top of that hill. We stand at the edge of a cliff. Is there a bridge? Can we find it? What new hill does it lead to?

* * *

There is a boy down the block Tom's 16–year-old sister Carrie is interested in.

"What does she say about me?" he asks Tom privately.

Tom's report is long, detailed, and less than accurate.

His sister is devastated.

Tom knows he has done something wrong but he isn't sure what.

* * *

"He earned it," Tom's cross country coach insists as he talks to Monica. "He met all the requirements."

As a ninth-grader Tom was on the freshman football team and JV wrestling team. His sophomore year he returned to a Special Olympics volleyball team and competed there. As a junior he ran JV track for the school.

Now, his senior year, he has been a member of the cross country team and, while never among the fastest runners, he has completed every race. According to the criteria established by the coach, Tom has earned a varsity letter.

His new jacket is red with white leather sleeves.

He seldom takes it off.

* * *

"I don't think a curtain will work," I say to Tom and his 13–year-old brother Andy. "I think you need a wall."

They nod.

The two share a small bedroom that has shrunk even more as both boys have grown. (And accumulated more priceless junk.) Fights have broken out.

Together we put up a 2–by–4 frame and a plywood barrier 6 feet high and 8 feet long.

The boys can't decide if their new living areas are "cubicles" or "cells."

They don't really care. Each enjoys the added privacy.

* * *

Carrie turned 16 and got her driver's license. My sister gave her an old car. Tom walks. Tom rides his 10–speed bike. Tom, on occasion, takes the bus.

Someone at school has given Tom a driver's education book. Every so often he digs it out, looks through it, and talks of getting his license.

We can't stop him, he says. He's 18.

I think of this kid who is so careful with the power mower and the gas weed trimmer and I have no problem with the idea.

I think of this kid whose temper can flare so suddenly, whose judgment can be so off, and I cringe.

Monica and I tell Tom we hope some day he is able to get his driver's license. Maybe when he's a little older. When he has a job and can pay for his own insurance. We try to explain to him how much it costs to own a car but he's not convinced.

Carrie's car needs some repairs. She spends $500 in two weeks.

For a while, Tom quits talking about getting his license or getting a car.

* * *

Tom takes a girl—a girl, he explains, who is a friend, not a girl friend—to the school's winter ball. Because he can't drive, his mom and I will be the chauffeurs. We'll take them to a restaurant and then to the school. After the dance, we'll pick them up.

At the restaurant, Monica and I are careful to request our table is nowhere near theirs.

Tom is the perfect gentleman. Handing her a corsage. Opening doors for her. Complimenting her on her dress.

* * *

Tom is taking a "Quick Cuisine" course at school. One afternoon he comes home and pulls a "pizza sandwich" from his coat pocket.

It's some kind of bread wrapped around tomato sauce, cheese and pepperoni. "I made a extra one for Carrie and Andy," he explains.

They slice it in half and devour it.

"When I come visit you at your apartment," Carrie says with food still in her mouth, "you can make these for me."

* * *

Monica and I didn't know if the idea of Tom living on his own was a realistic goal or only a dream. Now we suspect—we hope—he will be able to get that apartment. To hold down that job that pays enough to meet his expenses.

We're sure he will always need help balancing his budget. Getting bills paid on time. Keeping track of financial matters.

Not really dependent. Not really independent.

At this point we see Tom as leading an interdependent life. Relying on the strengths of others to help in the areas where he is weak.

I think about the help my parents and Monica's parents have provided for both of us over the years. The help from our siblings. From our friends.

I realize we all lead lives that are interdependent to one degree or another. Acts of kindness and generosity, support given and received, are parts of the mosaic that makes up each of our lives. Parts of the mosaic that makes each life unique. Each life the treasure that it is.

Bill Dodds is a full-time freelance writer who lives in the Seattle suburb of Mountlake Terrace. Among the more than a dozen books Bill has had published is My Sister Annie *(Boyds Mills Press), a middle-grade novel about an 11–year-old boy whose older sister has Down syndrome.*

Confessions of a Parent/Professional

Milton Seligman

Lori is twenty-three years old and lives with her mother about a mile and a half from my wife and me. Her sister, Lisa, is twenty-five years old and lives in a West Coast city. She moved there to make her way in the world after graduating from college with an anthropology degree.

For the past two years, Lori has worked as an assistant child care worker in a local hospital. Although her hours and days fluctuate, a typical day for her is to work from 7:30 a.m. to noon. She makes her way to and from the hospital by bus—often stopping on the way home to lunch at a Wendy's or to browse in Shadyside, a chic shopping area near her home. If the inclination hits her, Lori sometimes goes to Squirrel Hill to the Jewish Community Center for a Center Folk meeting to swim, or simply to "hang." Or she goes home to have lunch, to take care of the family dog "Paws," and watch the soaps. When time permits, she meets me for lunch close to the university where I teach or we both take a day off to see a movie and eat out for lunch or dinner. We are in touch by phone every couple of days and she visits us and her grandmother who lives nearby several times a month.

Often, unbeknownst to her mother or me, she will call a local agency or T.V. station to volunteer her services. She has volunteered at the Great T.V. Auction at WQED, the local PBS affiliate, the Macabee Games at the Jewish Community Center, the Hand-in-Hand Festival at the University of Pittsburgh, and for the county in their programs for persons with physical disabilities. If you haven't gathered by now, Lori is a young lady who loves to be around people and has an irrepressible independent streak. Her predominant strength is her sociability and a work ethic that I envy.

First Information

My recollection of the early days is more selective than that of Lori's mother. I am not blessed with a particularly acute memory for detail. I'm better at forests than trees. Furthermore, I suspect that denial has helped me cover painful emotions during the early years. The way I see it, Lori's mother was better at being "in touch" with her emotions, which may have motivated me to take a more stoic stance. This dynamic reminds me of the underfunctioning/overfunctioning that occurs in marriages. The more mom frets about a child's development, the more dad assumes a cool, "we can handle it" approach. The more dad becomes anxious about being on time for appointments, the more mom acts casually and unconcerned about this social transgression. It's predictable: when dad is overly anxious about something, mom will adopt a calmer attitude, perhaps in the interest of balance or to help lessen anxiety between parents.

There were no signs of a birth defect or other problems at birth. Lori's development over her first year of life was relatively unremarkable. However, at about one year of age we became concerned about her lack of development in certain areas. We communicated our concerns to our pediatrician. His response was to assure us that Lori was within normal developmental limits and that we should not be concerned. As weeks grew into months, our concerns grew. We became impatient with our pediatrician because we sensed that something was wrong and, because of our uneasiness about Lori's development, we switched doctors. Our new physician recommended that Lori have a battery of neurological and psychological tests at Children's Hospital. One of our concerns at that time was that Lori hadn't made any effort to walk and the test results from Children's indicated that there was "something abnormal" on her spine that may prevent her from walking—ever! This was a shocking disclosure—one that was communicated first to Lori's mother and then to me.

The doctor's disclosure about Lori's spine led to the following disquieting thoughts: As Lori grows older, how will we physically manage her and meet her physical needs? Will she be in a wheelchair? What will others think of us? Will Lori be pitied? And so on. Mostly I felt fear for the future and what Lori's condition would mean for her and the family.

I believe that parents of children with disabilities recall early events (especially around diagnostic information) with searingly vivid memories—some good and

some bad. These recollections should inform professionals who provide services to family members that they
must be on their very best behavior so that their memories of interactions with professionals are positive. Furthermore, I believe that a professional's response and
attitude toward children with disabilities plays some role
in how parents perceive their own children. Contrast a
professional's cold and distant demeanor with one who
is warm and accepting of the child and parents and is realistically optimistic and encouraging about the future.
Professionals' dealings with parents should be honest yet
kind, open, and communicative. They should be willing
to "be with" you during the difficult diagnostic disclosure stage and not abruptly depart after communicating
the diagnosis because this is difficult for them too. Gentle honesty is important but prognostic statements based
on ambiguous data should not be offered during the
early stages.

In writing about how professionals should behave
during the very early interactions between family members and professionals, I realize that I have offered a
more professional than a personal perspective. Please excuse this one and a few other mini-editorials that follow.
These excursions are borne out of personal experience
and the experience of other fathers. I feel strongly about
these issues and because of that I am moved to climb
onto the nearest soapbox.

In regard to Lori's walking, there is a story I must
tell. Lori crawled all over the house. When she sat on
the floor she did so with her legs flaccidly crossed, even
when she was in a chair. She never made any effort to
stand up or walk and I was beginning to despair about
her ability to ever do so. One day while her mother was

cooking and I was playing on the living room floor with her, I decided to lift Lori, prop her against a wall in the living room, cross over to the opposite wall, and said, "Lori, come over here to Daddy." To my shock and indescribable joy, Lori walked over to me and fell into my arms. She has walked ever since. My feet didn't touch the ground for weeks after that milestone event.

I tell this story because I believe that as fathers we are so close to our children that we often fail to consider the possibility that they may have some undiscovered talent or skill. To me this means that it is important to free our minds of our children's limitations as we know them and gently urge them and challenge them to try something different. I am convinced that Lori could have walked earlier if I had been more open-minded and concentrated less on what she could not do.

In addition to the concerns about her physical wellbeing, Lori received a diagnosis of Minimal Brain Dysfunction, an ambiguous, nondescript term that, after hearing tortured explanations of what it meant from professionals, seemed to mean that Lori was mildly retarded. However, any definitive prognostic implications of her condition could not be made due to her young age and because of her "borderline" diagnosis. Looking back I am very appreciative of the fact that the professionals did not offer a prognosis in the face of her ambiguous diagnosis. I know from other parents that they were not so lucky. In some cases, their child's disability was pronounced to be severe and unchangeable and they were encouraged to institutionalize their child. I have often felt that professionals sometimes advise parents according to their own attitudes, prejudices, and values and not what is best for the child and the family.

During the assessment period, I was filled with anger and frustration at not being able to get first-hand information. While Lori was in Children's there were no appointments set up with us. The medical staff involved in the assessment process "dropped in" at their convenience. More often than not, Lori's mother was there to meet with the physicians and other professionals and I rarely had the opportunity to get information first hand. It frustrated me to not be included in on these meetings and to not be able to ask questions. I was mostly angry at the professional staff but I recall being angry with my wife for not asking the "right questions." Sometimes I feel that our own anxieties as fathers turn into anger at innocent people.

I tried to make visits to the hospital during the time of day when the staff had met with Lori's mother in previous days. I remember feeling paranoid that the doctors appeared to be more at ease with Lori's mother than with me and that they intentionally avoided me. Actually, this observation runs counter to some research that suggests that physicians prefer to talk with fathers because they are perceived as more rational, less emotional, and easier to deal with.

I realize now that my paranoia during Lori's hospitalization was fueled by my anxiety and fear. Nevertheless, this experience leads me to conclude that professionals should make every effort to meet with both parents. Some of the initial turmoil that family members experience during the "first information" period can be lessened by meeting with the family instead of with just the mother or just the father.

Lisa

A concern that has plagued me since Lori was a toddler is how her disability will affect her sister Lisa. First-born and about two years older than Lori, Lisa has a more spirited personality than her younger sib. As a sib she had a close-up view of how others treated Lori and how she was treated by others as Lori's sister. During the early years, Lori was a neighborhood favorite—she was a cuddly, calm child adored by everyone. My fear at that time was that Lori was getting all of the positive attention and for Lisa to get her share, she had to engage in negative behaviors that got both my attention and anger. Since I was a young and inexperienced parent, Lisa got more of my negative attention than she deserved, yet even then I was aware that she needed more positive attention from me due to the adulation that Lori received. Her temper tantrums made it difficult for me at times to provide her with what she needed, although I learned and matured as a father and coped better over time. I felt guilty about that then and still do although my love and caring for Lisa was deep-rooted and our relationship grew over the years.

As Lori grew to pre-adolescence and adolescence her deficiencies became more obvious and the adulation she basked in earlier was replaced by a certain amount of scorn and rejection. The kids congregating in the neighborhood cul-de-sac played with her only if others were unavailable. Although a few of the neighborhood children seemed to be fond of her, I was aware that some children chronically taunted her and referred to her as "slow" and a "retard." My feelings toward these children became very negative and I would ignore them when I played with the kids in the cul-de-sac. Knowing something about individual differences, societal attitudes toward persons with disabilities and prejudice, I could understand their feelings, nevertheless I still disliked them for it. My dislike for them grew when I began to notice the bind these social interactions created for Lisa.

As Lori's sib, Lisa had to make instantaneous decisions about whether she was going to side with her sister or the neighborhood kids. If she sided with her sister, Lisa jeopardized her friendship with the other kids and, if she supported Lori, I wondered whether she was angry at her pals and angry toward Lori for being different and threatening her friendships. This must have been an insufferable bind.

I often observed the kids interacting from our living room window. My heart ached to see either Lisa or Lori hurt. I felt impotent to help either one avoid the pain although, on occasion, I would call the kids in so that they could escape the conflicts. I see now that by forcing Lisa to come in with her sister I didn't respect her already well-developed ability to cope with this situation. My behavior also probably reinforced and magnified the differences between my children and their playmates. I am continually amazed at how children overcome their fathers' occasional bad judgment and mistakes.

Although I'm sure that they were suffering from the rejection they felt, I now know that I called them into the house because of my own anguish. It's very hard to know how to negotiate this type of situation when it is happening. I realize that all children agonize over peer acceptance and rejection but I felt that what my daughters were forced to endure was particularly cruel. As I said, I had anger at the other children but also toward their parents. The difficult choices that Lisa had to make as a child and adolescent has forced her to examine what her ultimate feelings would be toward her sister.

One often hears that people endure and become strengthened by adversity. I should have known that from my parents, who are survivors of the Holocaust. In addition to surviving that horror, they endured the pain of losing their first-born child to a misdiagnosed case of appendicitis and of my early onset of rheumatoid arthritis. So it comes as no surprise to me that Lisa, being of the same stock, has grown up to be a young lady able to cope with life's vicissitudes. She is blessed with a warm, empathic personality and has a deep affection for her sister. It does not surprise me that research has shown that sibs of brothers and sisters with disabilities demonstrate great tolerance of others.

An interesting fact about sibling relationships, expressed by Tom Powell and Peggy Ogle (1985), is that: "Siblings provide a continuing relationship from which there is no annulment" (p. 12). As such I believe that parents of children with disabilities need to make every effort to lay the groundwork for positive sibling relationships, especially because these relationships survive their parents.

Divorce

There isn't much written on divorce in families of children with disabilities. What information exists suggests that divorce rates among these families are comparable to families with children who do not have disabilities. The issue of divorce in the disability literature is infrequently addressed even though divorce occurs in approximately half of married couples. When reading accounts from parents I sometimes get the impression that a child with a disability draws family members together, even when family tensions existed before the child's birth. I agree that this happens in some families, but I doubt that a troubled marriage improves its functioning after the birth of a child, disabled or not.

I believe that one needs to be careful about attributing marital conflict or divorce to the presence of a child with special needs. The decision to dissolve a marriage is a complex one, made up of personal styles and values, family of origin issues, external factors, and the like.

After much self searching, I feel in my heart that Lori's special circumstances had little to do with my divorce. However, I do believe that the aftermath of the separation and subsequent divorce affected both of my daughters. The impact of it on Lori was immediate and pronounced. She was distraught that her father no longer resided in the house and that she had to visit me in another residence. She seemed more sad than angry at the time (Lori was 13). Lori seemed to believe that the separation was a temporary arrangement and that her parents would eventually come together again. This reaction is not unusual among children and young adolescents. Although Lisa seemed to believe that the marriage was irretrievably broken early on, Lori voiced her fantasy that her father would someday return and resume his role in the family.

It is virtually impossible to speculate how the divorce affected my daughters over the long run. I believe that both of them have resolved this issue to a large extent but I feel that Lori's more immediate response allowed her to grapple with the dissolution of the family earlier and more completely than Lisa. In some ways

Lisa is still responding to the divorce—more by her actions and behavior than in words.

I'm not entirely certain why I choose to write about the divorce. I suppose that it is because of an uncomfortable sense that my daughters may have had an easier road had the family stayed intact. I still feel guilty about this but I do find some solace in the knowledge that both parents remained intimately involved with both children.

In general, though, I would like to see researchers investigate divorce in families where there is a child with a disability. I would also encourage parents who have experienced divorce speak to this issue in public forums and in their writings. My suspicion is that the general public believes that a child with a disability creates enormous tensions within the family, eventually culminating in divorce. On the other hand, parents who speak and write about their experience with their child project the notion that a child with a disability marshals constructive forces within the family system and actually brings family members together.

My guess is that the truth probably falls somewhere between what the general public seems to believe and what some parents have projected in their public utterances and in their writings. We need to openly address this issue so that the public is better informed and that parents who have experienced divorce are not filled with guilt and shame due to the perception that most other families are actually brought closer.

Changed Directions

Writing this essay has prompted me to examine how Lori has affected my life. In some fundamental ways Lori's presence hasn't changed it. Even in high school I championed the causes of the underdog. I've spoken against prejudice toward people who are "different" according to our society's bizarre standards of normality.

Although I experienced some career indecision in college, I finally chose psychology as an undergraduate student, rehabilitation counseling for my masters, and counseling psychology for my doctoral concentration. Both psychology and rehabilitation have strong humanistic foundations, so these areas of study fit my predisposition.

Looking back, I am not puzzled by my attitudes toward individual differences as I have always considered myself deviant from mainstream American society. My "differentness" and experience is an amalgamation of being German-born, Jewish, a son of Holocaust survivors, and having a chronic illness. Because of this history I can easily identify with minority group status. Therefore, Lori's arrival did not change my thinking in any fundamental way. I've often wondered how parents with disdain toward minorities and persons with disabilities philosophically cope with their child with a disability.

Lori was born several years after I graduated from my doctoral studies. Even though I had an interest in rehabilitation, my research and clinical work was in more traditional psychology and counseling areas. My doctoral dissertation was in the area of group psychotherapy.

Although to this day I have continued my interests in group therapy and other areas germane to mainstream psychology, there was a major addition to my interests after Lori's birth. As I mentioned earlier, I was anxious about how Lori's presence would affect our family. I surmised that other families may have had similar fears and, as an outgrowth of this, I became curious about how families cope with childhood disability. As a result, I read and began to write in the "family and disability" area to the extent that it became a major academic focus.

In choosing this area of concentration I again felt in the minority. Although professionals from nursing, medicine, social work, and special education have made contributions to this area of study, psychology was poorly represented. This was particularly true in the 1970s and 1980s but has changed somewhat in the present decade. In regard to my consuming involvement in family response to childhood disability, I sometimes wonder whether this academic interest shielded me from more personal insights, fears, and emotions into my own coping. Writing about research studies and the personal observations of other family members tends to objectify a subject so that it feels like I am dealing with a foreign subject that does not touch me personally. What supports this observation is the recognition that writing this essay is considerably more difficult and painful for me than writing an article for a professional journal on the same topic. To sum up, Lori's presence in my life has had little impact on my fundamental values but it has had a dramatic effect on my professional life.

The Future

I believe that all fathers worry about the future when it comes to their offspring. However, fathers of children with disabilities worry even more because our children have fewer opportunities for success, they may be restricted in their ability to function independently, and because we perceive our children to be more vulnerable. It is for these reasons that the future is so worrisome to me.

I mentioned earlier that Lori can function independently in many respects. However, she has not had the experience of living independent of both parents. She has a limited understanding of the responsibilities that come with independent or semi-independent living. Lori's experience in managing a residence and to some extent coping with financial responsibilities is limited. I sense that she feels increasingly less willing to live apart from both parents the older she gets. This causes great anxiety in me because I fear that she will have difficulty negotiating a more independent life if her parents are unable to help her ease into this necessary life transition.

Tears come to my eyes when I think of Lori without her parents. She is so accustomed to having them around. I try to suppress the apprehension that wells up in me when thoughts of Lori's future come to mind. But I can't deny the reality that anxieties about Lori's future are relentless. I am, however, comforted when I think about how Lori has been active and creative in developing a life for herself. She has shown remarkable resourcefulness in negotiating life thus far. This gives me hope that she will be as adaptable when it comes time to leave the "nest." Although it is hard to "let go" as parents, the fact that community living arrangements are difficult to come by delays the inevitable separation process. In the Pittsburgh community one is more apt to secure semi-independent living when a child is in a crisis situation or has severe or multiple disabilities.

I want to close this essay by saying that Lori's development to date has far exceeded my expectations. I am a proud father of a young adult who leads an active and varied life and has coped admirably with what life has dealt her.

―――――――――――

Milton Seligman lives in Pittsburgh, Pennsylvania, where he is a professor in the Department of Psychology in Education. At the University, he teaches courses on counseling skills, group therapy, and disability and the family. He is involved in training counselors at the masters degree level and psychologists at the doctoral level. Milt has written, co-authored, and edited several books; among them are, Ordinary Families, Special Children *(with Rosalind Darling), the second edition of* The Family with a Handicapped Child, *and, with Laura Marshak,* Counseling Persons with Physical Disabilities. *In addition to his teaching and writing duties he maintains a part-time private practice in Pittsburgh.*

Life's Illusions

Charles A. Hart

I've looked at life from both sides now,
from give and take and still, somehow,
it's life's illusions I recall,
I really don't know life at all.
                              —Joni Mitchell

My granddad had a story for everything. He ran a country store during Montana's homesteading days. Granddad must have spent a good deal of time at the post office counter, because he seemed to know every piece of Western folk-lore by heart. I suppose he picked up his stories hanging around farmers and cattlemen in the days before television, back when people still talked for entertainment.

One of granddad's favorites was the one about the farmer who was a gamblin' fool. It seemed this farmer would take any bet. Finally, he made a crazy wager: he could lift a full-grown steer. He added just one condi-

tion to his wager. He wanted eighteen months to prove
up before settling. On his way home, he bought a preg-
nant cow. He figured she'd deliver soon and he could
pick up her calf. The farmer knew he could lift a newborn. He'd done it before and expected he could lift it
the second day, too. The calf might gain a few pounds a
day, but he reasoned his strength might grow at the
same rate, *as long as he kept picking up the calf*. Granddad said the farmer went out to the corral every morning, just to lift that calf. The calf kept getting heavier and
the farmer—well, he just strained a little harder every
day.

Granddad never finished this tale or told anyone
how it was supposed to end. He just grinned and let the
listeners draw their own conclusions. He figured the
imagination was more powerful than any punch line. He
just left us thinking about that farmer.

As a child, I wanted to know this story's outcome. I
bet against the farmer. His reasoning seemed absurd: No
man could gain strength as fast as a steer gains weight.
Common sense says this experiment won't work. He'll
break his back trying! On the other hand, why not? The
farmer wants a chance, his long-shot for a miracle. Let
him try. No one doubts he could keep up with the calf's
growth for a few days, maybe even weeks . . . so why
not longer? There are so many examples of adjustment
and accommodation in the world, it's hard to see
boundaries to reality or to keep up with technology's
frontiers. Why shouldn't we believe in the impossible?
How much can a person accomplish with faith and perse-
verance?

Imagine the farmer eighteen months later. His gam-
bling buddies have joined him at the corral, waiting to

see him fail or break his fool back. They grow quiet as
he parades into the corral, a full-grown steer on his lead.
As the others gape in astonishment, he proudly hoists
the animal and collects his bets.

Today, I like this second ending. It raises possibilities above predictions, a belief that dreams can come
true and that people are stronger than they think. This
interpretation means more to me than the harsher one.
It helps me understand my own life and the challenge of
living with two generations of autism.

My attitude about the disability began in the 1940s.
As the youngest child, I watched others conceal my
brother at home. By the age of four, I knew Scott was
our secret, an embarrassment we sent to a back bedroom
when company came. His pain and the pain of him were
too private to share with others. My sisters and I left as
soon as we could, marrying young or attending college
across the country. Years later, I would hear a psychologist classify our behavior as "siblings' flight." It was
flight all right, but Scott hadn't chased us away. Fear,
shame, and confusion had made our home unbearable.

We didn't hate Scott, our gentle, high-strung
brother who grew old at home while his younger sisters
and brother went off to school. We cursed the disability,
but not him. Somehow in the family mythology, we confused the person with the condition, making Scott an excuse for all our disappointments: Dad's drinking, Mom's
seclusion, the family's financial worries. All these and
more we blamed on "his problem." In our imaginations,
he'd become our central problem, a master of chaos
keeping our lives in turmoil.

Early on, I thought Scott's disability was the worst
curse a family could suffer. I'd seen my parents break un-

der the burden and knew I couldn't follow. Could it happen again? Was it possible that I might father a "child who never grows up?" This fear plagued me in my twenties, but after five years of marriage, I knew I had to start a family or lose the woman I loved. She came from a "normal family," and expected to bear healthy children like her sisters, so I traded my nightmares for hopes. Placing our bet in the lottery of life, we conceived our first child.

At Ted's birth, I nagged the doctor for reassurance. "Had the kid passed all the tests?" "Was there a chance—even a small chance—that this perfectly formed infant had a flaw?" Ted passed every screening. In spite of a cesarean delivery, he earned a "nine" out of ten on the newborn scale. A real "winner," a champion in the delivery room!

Like most men, I didn't know much about babies. So, no one could compare with my first-born. Each move, every step and word, seemed early and brilliant! Precocious! I watched our little prodigy, the fruit of our loins, pass through his early stages of development. We enjoyed the infancy so much, we weren't in a hurry to see it pass. But, by Ted's second birthday, we noticed little "quirks," eccentricities that suggested he was different (but surely better!) than other children. His language was odd (maybe he didn't need to ask questions). He didn't play with other children (perhaps he liked adults better). His scores on developmental charts started to slip (maybe the charts were wrong).

By his third birthday, we confronted the truth; our son wasn't "advanced," not even "typical." He was *different* and it wasn't a *difference* we had chosen. No one would pick this *difference* out of a catalog. We hadn't received what we'd ordered. The perfect child hadn't arrived with full warranty, but he was *our* child, not to be returned and *not to be devalued!*

Like many parents, we suffered through a series of diagnoses that seemed more like professional guesses: "brain damaged," "neurologically impaired," and finally, "autistic," the adjective finally used to name Scott's problem. We searched for help, ways to "fix" Ted, but the more we learned, the less we hoped. We had so much stress in our home, our second child developed colic. It looked like my worst nightmare had come true; my second family seemed as doomed AS my first.

On the positive side, my wife and I had resources my parents had never known. We had steady employment, better education, and access to a university-based training center. Furthermore, society had begun to recognize the rights and needs of people with disabilities. Unlike Scott who'd been born in the 'twenties, my "child of the seventies" wouldn't have to stay home. The law guaranteed him an "appropriate" education. Medical understanding had progressed too. Doctors no longer blamed parents for the disability. The stigma was lifting like a cloud. We decided we'd never hide this child. We weren't ashamed of him!

It took awhile to overcome all the fears from my childhood, but new friendships in the ARC and the Autism Society helped me heal. We discovered we weren't alone, our son wasn't hopeless—and neither was my brother. Concern for my son's welfare made me more sensitive to my brother's feelings. I began to see Scott in another light, and the vision startled me. It seemed clearer, more honest, than my earlier view. All those years, we had overlooked Scott's needs. We were too eager to blame someone else for our problems.

Rehashing the past, I realized we had it all wrong: *Scott hadn't been "our problem"; we were his!* Confronting those feelings hurt, but the pain brought a rush of adrenaline and determination. It hit me like a bolt of lightning:

Whether something's a curse or a blessing depends on our interpretation.

I could choose to interpret my son's disability as I wanted. Will it be a burden, a challenge, or an opportunity? It was up to me: I had to play the hand I'd been dealt, but "how" was up to me!

During what seemed a long and tortuous childhood, my wife and I struggled to understand Ted and tried not to neglect his brother in the process. Having been Scott's brother, I could identify with my younger son's concerns, though he never spoke them. He craved a "normal" brother and worried through his adolescent quest for identity.

Raising two sons with such different needs put us to the test. We stumbled through their childhoods, waiting for graduation like light promised at the end of the tunnel. Ted's twenty-second birthday found us pretty well prepared. For years we'd worked toward this transition, his passage into the adult world. He'd graduate at the end of the year. Between his part-time jobs and an "S.S.I." check, he'd have a reasonable income. His supervisors knew him well and had trained him during student internships. We even fixed up a basement apartment for him and furnished it with entertainment options, a television, VCR, and Nintendo, and monthly reminders for the rent!

Generally satisfied, we thought everything was planned for graduation, but Ted didn't. That spring, in his senior year, he stretched his verbal skills to their limit. He caught us off guard with his announcement:

"I'm going to the prom."

He was going to the prom! He'd thought about it for years. At eighteen, he'd seen kids his own age plan their prom night. He watched the younger ones get ready again next year . . . and the year after that. And now, three years after his peers had graduated, Ted saw his last chance. No "ifs," "ands," or "buts" about it; he was going to the prom. All he needed was a date. That's about like saying "all Cinderella needs is a gown, coach, horses, and attendants."

He simply couldn't get a date on his own. Six feet tall with a square jaw and blond hair, he might pass for a "hunk" until opening his mouth. Then words or nonsense syllables can spill out, sometimes without planning or control. Other students laughed at him. Some of the cheerleaders called him "cute" and tolerated his attention at assemblies, but none would actually date him.

Ted could have asked another special education student, but he had typical cultural bias. Like most guys in his school, his idea of beauty had been shaped by television. He wanted a date that would "knock their eyes out," a tall blond who'd lean on his arm when he walked into the prom. Where do you find a woman like that? And, if you find her, how do you talk her into the date? No one wants to go to a strange prom with a tongue-tied escort.

Believe it or not, we pulled it off! A family friend, Miss Connecticut (1962) had a daughter less than a year older than our son. A striking blond, Jennifer attended graduate school on the east coast. She and Ted had already met through their families and, in spite of educational differences, they liked and trusted one another. Jennifer understood what prom night meant to Ted, so she agreed to take a formal out of storage and fly across the country.

As prom night approached, we helped Ted prepare. We wanted his experience to seem as "special" as we had believed ours was a generation ago. Ted didn't have friends who could advise him, so he put himself in our hands. We dusted off the etiquette book and the family tuxedo. It fit Ted better than me. He agreed to let me chauffeur him and Jennifer in the family car. Ted even planned their dinner before the dance. Only one detail remained, the floral tribute, *the corsage.*

In prom culture, the male always buys his date flowers. Jennifer had to wear flowers, and they had to come from Ted. It was a very tender symbol, because this young man might never have occasion to present a woman with flowers again. If I'd picked up the phone, I could have ordered that corsage in two minutes flat. But that would have taken the opportunity away from Ted. He needed that experience and I wanted him to have it. So, we did it the hard way. I prepared Ted to buy his date's flowers. Over the years I'd learned to do a "task analysis," breaking an experience down into small steps, then practicing them in sequence until we both knew Ted could perform independently.

First, we rehearsed Ted's interview with Jennifer, so that he could ask what color she planned to wear and whether she wanted flowers on her wrist or on her shoulder. Via long-distance, she told him she wanted a wrist corsage to accent a black dress. Next we researched flowers, using the encyclopedia. We looked at gardenias, roses, and orchids, noting their colors. Finally, Ted felt confident enough to make a choice.

Preparing for the trip to the florist, Ted wanted to do his "role plays." He likes to have a planned script. Practicing the words at home makes it easier to say them in another setting. Ted gave me the florist's role, so I invited him into my imaginary shop:

"Good afternoon. What can I do for you?"

"I want to buy a corsage," he answered.

"Not really." I interrupted to explain that, if he "bought" a corsage on Wednesday, it would look pretty stale and wilted on Saturday night. "You don't want to buy a corsage today, you want to order one," I prompted.

We rehearsed until Ted seemed letter perfect. Just for luck, I humored him, switching roles, so he could play florist while I impersonated him. When he had the script down pat, we strolled to our neighborhood florist, the "Pickety-Patch." As soon as the little bell on the door stopped jangling, Ted looked like he was trapped. The air was heavy with the smell of flowers and spice. Ted has always been hypersensitive to odors so this room got him wired. Sachets and floral extracts were everywhere, as well as vases, beakers, and planters sprouting different blooms. Colors, glass, and mirrors sparkled from every corner.

Near the back, a single clerk sorted through receipts and orders. Hearing the door, she stopped filing and turned her attention to us. I waited for Ted to speak, looking at him expectantly. It grew very quiet in the shop, then he cleared his throat. His entire body had grown rigid. He drew his face into a grimace and blurted out,

"I'm Ted. I'm here to rent the purple flowers."

The clerk looked startled. She glanced at me as I calmly prompted, "Let's try that again, Ted." He drew a couple of deep breaths and furrowed his brows. "Look at her and tell her what you want to order," I suggested.

Novelty and sensory over-stimulation had gotten the best of him. He stumbled a few more times before getting back on track. Finally, by staying calm and speaking slowly he was able to answer all of the clerk's questions:

He wanted a corsage for Saturday. His date wanted to wear it on her wrist. He preferred purple or lavender roses. He'd pay when he picked it up Saturday afternoon.

This conversation would have been natural, reflexive communication for most people. But Ted's disability made it perilous. Unfamiliar environments make him nervous. Besides, communication's always risky when a person responds to questions with pre-rehearsed answers. Ted's social stress and verbal confusion come from his neurological differences, subtle little accidents in the wiring of his body and brain. We know he experiences many things differently than the average person, but he'll never be able to tell us how his perception varies from ours. But after twenty-two years, I had grown accustomed to Ted's responses. I hadn't expected the clerk's reaction.

"You have a lot of patience," she said. "I could never be so patient."

At first bewildered, she had changed to sympathy, then to admiration. But she was admiring the wrong person! I didn't feel "special" for supporting Ted, but his progress . . . that was remarkable! Unknown to the clerk, this young man had climbed mountains of barriers and swam oceans of confusion, just to reach this point. Saturday night wouldn't find him working a jigsaw puzzle as his uncle had spent his youth. Ted was going to the prom!

Back home from the florist's, I told my wife about the experience. I recounted Ted's faltering "I'm here to rent the purple flowers," and my subsequent coaching. We were used to those situations, but not the saleswoman's response. I'd never thought of myself as "patient." Quite the contrary. In school I'd always been a "fast learner," impatient to the point of intolerance. When classmates didn't grasp ideas as quickly as myself, I'd been restless, quick to judge and eager to feel superior. I had many goals as a younger man, but patience wasn't one of them. It shocked me to hear a stranger say, "You have a lot of patience."

"No!" I'd wanted to shout. "This isn't 'patience,' this is 'understanding.'" There was so much I might have told her, if she'd been interested. My son, not I, deserved credit for patience. My neurological system works. It transmits signals instantaneously from memory bank to impulse center to vocal cords and back. Ted has to labor the pathways we take for granted. He might "blow it" from time to time, but he keeps struggling upstream, towards a life the rest of us take for granted. It amazed me that someone would call me "patient" instead of admiring my son's greater patience and fortitude.

My wife brought me back to reality, pointing out
that the clerk's response had been more "normal" than
either Ted's or mine. She pointed out that, over time
and without realizing it, I'd developed listening skills
that looked like "patience" to others. She reminded me
that others don't see our relationship in context. TheY
don't see the history and the struggle, only the first impression, the "here and now."

Maybe I look "patient" after all.

Twenty years ago I didn't expect anyone to call me
"patient." But I didn't think I could cope with a son's disability, either. I had predicted the worst, thinking the
burden would break me. It had never occurred to me
that I could become a stronger person, that I would discover meaning and direction for my own life through
the challenge of another person. I hadn't done anything
extraordinary, just lifted my calf each day. Granddad
was right not to finish the story. He knew the ending depends on the listener. We write our own endings. If you
want that farmer to win his wager, he will!

Prom night I dropped Ted and Jennifer at the dance
and gave them taxi fare for the ride back. At home we
phoned my father-in-law, letting him know that his most
handsome grandson had gone to the prom. Then I called
a sister in Albuquerque. I knew she'd understand. We
talked about our brother's stunted life and the amazing
progress Ted had already made. We cried.

I keep a photo from the dance on my desk. Jennifer
stands beside Ted. On her wrist she wears a corsage of
lavender roses. That image freezes June 6, 1992 in time.
Prom night can mean a lot to people. Some events sym-
bolize a long process like education or courtship and
condense it into a photo opportunity. In clothes de-

signed for the occasion, people can be what they want to be. At that moment, their dreams have come true. Clothes, flowers, and smiles camouflage their everyday identities. Snap! The camera records the illusion. Snap! It becomes a document.

My son looked great the night of June 6th, 1992. I'm proud of that image, but I owe him more than pride. Before I knew he faced special challenges, I had fairly typical ambitions for my son. I hoped my children would be better, more successful versions of my wife and myself. That wasn't a very exciting goal, but comfortable, normal. I couldn't predict that he'd wrench me from the mainstream and lead me in a more interesting direction, his personal path.

To keep up with Ted I had to slow down. He taught me that some people need more time. They don't all accelerate under stress or perform under pressure. He's given me one of the best lessons a writer could learn: *Words aren't always the answer!* In fact, words sometimes increase misunderstanding, instead of relieving it. Conversations with Ted remind me I should write more clearly, show more respect for the communication process. I should understand its risks and pitfalls . . . because Ted showed me.

When my son was very young, he was easy to lift. It seemed appropriate to make decisions for him, choosing clothes, scheduling activities, setting behavior rules. I'd bargained for that responsibility and it never tweaked my conscience to tell a ten-year-old to eat what's on his plate. It's harder now. Not because Ted's heavier (that's another tale), it's because *my conscience* is heavier. I think a twenty-three-year-old guy is as entitled to freedom of choice and expression as I am. So, whenever I try to influence him, shape consumer patterns or social behavior, I'd better be certain it's for his best interest, not my peace of mind.

Sometimes it's hard to recognize boundaries between this father's concerns and his son's desires. Isn't that life? Maybe we're not so different, after all. I'd like to think that we have a relationship similar to other fathers and sons, it's just more intense. Though I didn't volunteer for the privilege of being Ted's dad, the experience has been transforming!

Call it love.

Charles A. Hart is the author of A Parent's Guide to Autism *(Pocket Books, 1993) and* Without Reason: A Family Copes with Two Generations of Autism *(Harper & Row, 1989; Penguin, 1991). A former board member and vice-president of the Autism Society of America, Charles won the Society's Literary Award in 1990. Charles has worked for the University of Washington and the ARC of King County (Washington) and has volunteered in a variety of organizations serving people with disabilities. He received a Jefferson Award for Volunteer Service in Washington State in 1989.*

Life Goes On

Frank Burke

Sometimes when I see the people who run to my son, Christopher, seeking his autograph, I can't help but remember that there were actually a few times when people ran *away* from him. Life has taken an ironic turn for us, and the changes become more and more unbelievable.

The day Christopher was born, 28 years ago, started out wonderfully. But within hours, my wife, Marian, and I became devastated and confused. Marian called me from the hospital and, between sobs, said, "Frank, the pediatrician told me we have a 'mongoloid' and nothing can be done about it." I rushed back to the hospital and tearfully listened to her relate how the doctor bluntly recommended that we seriously consider putting Christopher in an institution. He said that handling him would put a strain on the whole family. Our decision was easy to make: he was our baby, and he was coming home with us.

A few days later, we left the hospital without our beautiful blond-haired baby; Christopher stayed behind for more genetic testing. Resentfully, Marian signed a statement saying she would return to claim her child. On our weary trip home, two thoughts raced through our minds: what was "mongolism," and why us?

Our faith in God got us through the first six months: it was then that we told our three other children. Ellen, 16, said, "So what?" Anne, 14, and J.R., 11, chimed in, "He's no different from other babies we've seen." In due time, we discussed Christopher's condition with our relatives and they accepted him with open arms. He was invited to all family celebrations, and this support made our life much easier.

Christopher loved his first school, The Kennedy Child Study Center in New York City. The next school he attended was Cardinal Cushing School and Training Center in Hanover, Massachusetts. I'll never forget when we took him for a trial visit—he unknowingly destroyed me.

We had been reluctant to leave him at the school, but two of the nuns assured us that Christopher would be fine. Marian hugged and kissed him good-bye. Then it was my turn: I bent down to put my arms around him, but he stood ram-rod straight and, with the wisdom of an eight-year-old, said, "Dad, big boys don't hug and kiss. They just shake hands." When I got to our car I broke down and cried. I wondered, were we doing the right thing? But Christopher loved Cardinal Cushing, and he made good educational strides. He spent five years there, coming home for long weekends and summers.

For seven years after that, he went to Don Guanella School in Springfield, Pennsylvania, where he was close to J.R.'s home and family, Not having him such a distance from family made it easier on everyone.

Over the years, Christopher flew home from Boston and took the train back from Pennsylvania. This constant traveling added to Christopher's self-reliance, but it often made me a wreck. When he flew, I was concerned about bad weather and when he rode the train, I envisioned him getting off at the wrong stop or getting lost at the station. But he never had any problems. In fact, he turned his arrivals into a game by somehow missing us at the agreed-upon meeting place—and then having us paged. I never knew his secret, but he managed to pull it off almost every time. He became a skilled traveler, and I became a skilled worrier.

That was just one change Christopher brought out in me. His entrance into my life also made me a more tolerant person. My military service, followed by a career in the New York City Police Department, made me accustomed to regulations and procedures. I subscribed to the belief that "black is black, white is white." But when Christopher came along, he taught me that there *are* gray areas. I now believe that people aren't "abled" or "disabled"—they only have different measures of ability.

When Hollywood beckoned, Christopher and I headed west. We could not predict how successful Corky Thacher and "Life Goes On" would be, so Marian stayed in New York. She had a wonderfully interesting job as the manager of the National Stationery Show. Meanwhile, Christopher and I became the Odd Couple in our two-bedroom apartment in Burbank, near the Warner Brothers' Studios. I was the cook, the maid, the chauffeur, and the valet, but most of all, Christopher's pal in his new career.

During filming in the first season, I had no idea how personally I was involving myself in Christopher's character. When Corky had to be sad, happy, or confused—unbeknownst to me—I was mimicking his every emotion off-camera. When I realized what I was doing, I retreated to his trailer and worked on his fan mail and telephone messages. (This, by the way, is a task that never ends. Numerous organizations want Christopher's help to make personal appearances, place phone calls, write letters, or send a photo. It's primarily up to Marian and myself to handle these constant requests.)

It was during the first season of "Life Goes On" that I became aware of Chris's determination to succeed. J.R. had given him a framed motto, which hung on his wall at home and in his room on the "Life Goes On" set. It read, "Obstacles are what you see when you take your eyes off the goal." Christopher had made that his personal motto, and I couldn't have been prouder of him. Twelve- and fourteen-hour days are the norm in filming a one-hour television drama, but he never complained and no filming time was lost because of him. Christopher told me about Spencer Tracy's credo: "Dad, Tracy said, 'A good actor knows his lines, gets to the set on time and hits his mark.' That's what I will do." And that is exactly what he strove to do.

We would take turns picking the restaurants and movies, but our interests were almost never the same. I remember reluctantly going to see "La Bamba" and "The Buddy Holly Story." I had made up my mind before we got to the theater: "I'll go but I won't like it." Lo and behold, I often thoroughly enjoyed his choices. Yes, Christopher was teaching me, in his subtle way.

We did, however, have our battles. I would get after him about the neatness of his room, his penchant for collecting magazines and music and video tapes, his ability to watch the same movies over and over again and for losing track of time. And I was still advising him about what clothes to wear and how to spend his money. Finally, I realized my structured background made me rigid. I knew I had to relax and let go of the reins I held on Chris, and I feel I have succeeded, although I'm told I occasionally slip back to my old habits.

"Life Goes On" lasted for four years and we are now back living in New York. Christopher has had no problem in adjusting. He works three days a week for the National Down Syndrome Society. He often visits P.S. 138, a city-wide school for children with multiple disabilities. He proudly recalls that he got his first job there as an elevator operator before becoming an actor. Since "Life Goes On," he has appeared in an episode of "The Commish" and in the six-hour miniseries, "Heaven and Hell."

As for me, I've been retired since March, 1987 and I have never been busier. My day starts early, negotiating details (along with Marian) regarding the many requests for Christopher's time. As Christopher's manager, I accompany him to every function he attends. Marian, Christopher, and I have been to Spain, Germany, Malta, and Canada, and have criss-crossed the U.S. countless times. Christopher is a spokesperson for both The National Down Syndrome Society and The National Down Syndrome Congress. In addition to their functions, we make a point to go to the events put on by the three spe-

cial schools he attended. With all his fame, Christopher
has not changed; he has not "gone Hollywood" on us.
He never fails to glowingly acknowledge us and the rest
of his family when he appears at these events.

I don't want to give the idea that everything was perfect for Chris growing up. He got roughed up and suffered at the hands of unthinking individuals. He had a
serious lung operation as the result of a schoolmate pushing a pine branch into his mouth. He was struck by a hit-
and-run cab driver. And there were times when people
chose to stay away from him.

When he was about five, I came home from work
one evening to find Marian in tears. She told me, "Chris
was in the playground and ran over to a group of young
children and their mothers. He joined right in. I was
watching from the window. The mothers snatched their
children up and went to another area of the playground.
Chris was left by himself. I had to go down and take him
home. Frank, how could they be so mean? He doesn't
have a contagious disease." Throughout the years, we
have tried to do the best we can with the cards that life
has dealt us. Our faith and our family have been our
strength.

In the 28 years since we were first faced with the
situation, much progress has been made in welcoming babies with challenges. If I had to give advice, I'd strongly
recommend that fathers utilize their families for support
and join a group in their area. Early intervention programs are prevalent—seek the assistance they offer.
Don't hesitate to bring your children with you whenever
it is possible.

But I'm not speaking as an expert; I can only say
what worked for our family. In our situation, there was

no structured participation on my part. When I could, I attended functions, and at other times I did the household chores, freeing my wife to guide Christopher. I must state that the planning for Christopher's education was accomplished by Marian, because I was busy with my career as a New York City police officer. I was also trying to obtain my college degree in criminal justice. (I wanted to graduate before my oldest child, Ellen.)

I knew Marian was far more capable in obtaining the best possible education for our son. She has always had a caring and understanding way about her. She sees the good in people and recognizes that people with challenges have to overcome conditions they were born with. She envisions them living in two worlds: the world of other people who also face challenges and the cruel, unyielding, "normal" world.

Fathers have a responsibility to prepare their children for that demanding world. I made it a family project to teach Christopher good table manners and to be courteous and polite. He made sure he was always neatly dressed, and we trained him to have good personal habits. Don't we do this for our other children? It is *so* important to do it for children with special needs. Yes, correcting Christopher was painful, but we knew it was necessary if he was to be socially accepted.

I now look back and see that what was sadness when Christopher was born has been, in reality, a blessing. Hard work and family unity resulted in a wonderful son who is a role model not only for people who have challenges, but for others as well. Nothing could make me prouder.

———————————————————

Francis D. Burke was born in New York City. As a gunner on a Flying Fortress during World War II, Frank was shot down, wounded, and became a prisoner of war in Stalag 17. He has been married for 46 years, has four children and ten grandchildren. He retired from the New York City Police Department as an Inspector after 30 years of service. Christopher keeps him busy, traveling with him all over the world on his speaking engagements and his continuing television career. The Burkes have a New York City apartment as well as a home on the south shore of Long Island.

About the Editor:

Donald J. Meyer is the director of the Sibling Support Project located at the Children's Hospital and Medical Center in Seattle, Washington. As director, he conducts workshops for family members and service providers across the country on issues concerning siblings of people with special needs. He also provides training for Sibshops—support and educational programs for school-age brothers and sisters.

He was a founder of SEFAM (Supported Extended Family Members) program at the University of Washington, which pioneered services for fathers, siblings, and grandparents. His publications include *Sibshops* (Paul H. Brookes, 1994), *The Fathers Program* (University of Washington Press, 1985), and *Living with a Brother or Sister with Special Needs: A Book for Sibs* (The University of Washington Press, 1985).

In 1994, he created the "Parenting Special Needs" topic on the Prodigy Parenting Bulletin Board, where he serves as a special contributor. Don and his wife, a special education preschool teacher, have four children, ages 6, 10, and twins born in 1994.